Wonderlic Test Practice Exams: Wonderlic Basic Skills Quantitative and Verbal Test Preparation Study Guide with 380 Questions and Answers

Wonderlic Test Practice Exams: Wonderlic Basic Skills Quantitative and Verbal Test Preparation Study Guide with 380 Questions and Answers

© COPYRIGHT 2017, 2020. Exam SAM Study Aids & Media dba www.examsam.com

ISBN: 978-1-949282-42-9

Note: Wonderlic and Wonderlic Basic Skills Test are registered trademarks of Wonderlic, Inc., which is not affiliated with and does not endorse these materials.

TABLE OF CONTENTS

Wonderlic Basic Skills Verbal Practice Test 1:

Answers and explanations:

FORMULA SHEET

Weight

1 ounce ≈ 28.350 grams
1 pound = 16 ounces
1 pound ≈ 453.592 grams
1 milligram = 0.001 grams
1 kilogram = 1,000 grams
1 kilogram ≈ 2.2 pounds
1 ton = 2,000 pounds

Volume

1 cup = 8 fluid ounces
1 quart = 4 cups
1 gallon = 4 quarts
1 gallon = 231 cubic inches
1 liter ≈ 0.264 gallons
1 cubic foot = 1,728 cubic inches
1 cubic yard = 27 cubic feet
1 board foot = 1 inch by 12 inches by 12 inches

Distance

1 foot = 12 inches
1 yard = 3 feet
1 mile = 5,280 feet
1 mile ≈ 1.61 kilometers
1 inch = 2.54 centimeters
1 foot = 0.3048 meters
1 meter = 1,000 millimeters
1 meter = 100 centimeters
1 kilometer = 1,000 meters
1 kilometer ≈ 0.62 miles

Area

1 square foot = 144 square inches
1 square yard = 9 square feet

Circle

number of degrees in circle = 360°
circumference ≈ 3.14 × *diameter*
area ≈ 3.14 × (*radius*)^2

Triangle

sum of angles = 180°
area = ½ (*base* × *height*)

Rectangle

perimeter = 2(*length* + *width*)
area = *length* × *width*

Rectangular Solid (Box)

volume = *length* × *width* × *height*

Cube

volume = (*length of side*)^3

Cylinder

volume ≈ 3.14 × (*radius*)^2 × *height*

Cone

volume ≈ (3.14 × *radius*^{2} ×

WONDERLIC BASIC SKILLS TEST FORMAT AND QUESTION TYPES

The Wonderlic Basic Skills Test contains 45 math and quantitative skills questions which you will need to answer in 20 minutes.

It also contains 50 verbal skills questions, for which you will be allowed an additional 20 minutes.

The questions will be multiple choice, with answer options provided. You should choose an answer even if you are not sure since there is no penalty for incorrect responses.

The questions on the Wonderlic Basic Skills Test can be placed into six broad categories: basic math computation, quantitative evaluation, algebra and geometry, reading and using information in various formats, recognizing word meanings, and identifying correct grammar and sentence construction.

You will see different types of questions in each of these six categories:

QUANTITATIVE SKILLS EXAM

Basic Math Computation
- Addition, subtraction, multiplication, and division
- Whole numbers
- Whole monetary units
- Whole units of measure (time, length, weight, and distance)

Math Computation with Quantitative Evaluation
- Addition, subtraction, multiplication, and division
- Whole numbers
- Whole monetary units
- Fractions and mixed numbers
- Fractional units of measure
- Comparisons of fractions
- Rates, proportions, and percentages
- Evaluation of graphs or other visual data representations

Algebra and Geometry
- Rates, proportions, and percentages
- Variable expressions and equations
- Lengths, angles, areas, and volume of geometric figures

VERBAL SKILLS EXAM

Locate, Understand, and Use Information in Various Formats
- Locating specific information in instructions, articles, and other texts
- Understanding instructions on how to carry out a process
- Using literature and other textual information

Recognize Word Meanings by Definition or Context
- Completing a sentence with an appropriate word
- Recognizing word meanings
- Identifying the correct use of words with multiple meanings
- Recognizing the meanings of potentially unknown words in the context of a sentence

Identify Correct Grammar and Sentence Construction
- Identifying a complete sentence
- Understanding agreement of grammatical subject and verb
- Recognizing correct sentence structure
- Completing complex and compound sentence constructions
- Identifying errors in sentence construction

You will see all of the above types of questions in this study guide.

Be sure to read the explanations for each question at the back of this publication to gain more strategies on how to answer each type of question on the exam.

WONDERLIC BASIC SKILLS QUANTITATIVE PRACTICE TEST 1

Basic Math and Math Computation with Quantitative Evaluation

1) $82 + 9 \div 3 - 5 = ?$
   A) −40.50
   B) 40.50
   C) 80.00
   D) 85.33

2) $52 + 6 \times 3 - 48 = ?$
   A) 22
   B) 82
   C) 126
   D) 322

3) What is the lowest common denominator for the following equation?
   $(^1/_3 + {}^{11}/_5) + (^1/_{15} - {}^4/_5)$
   A) 3
   B) 5
   C) 15
   D) 45

4) Convert the following to decimal format: 3/20
   A) 0.0015
   B) 0.015
   C) 0.15
   D) 0.66

5) 60 is 20 percent of what number?
   A) 80
   B) 120
   C) 1200
   D) 300

6) $6^3/_4 - 2^1/_2 = ?$
   A) $4^1/_4$
   B) $4^3/_8$
   C) $4^5/_8$
   D) $4^6/_8$

7) Which one of the values will correctly satisfy the following mathematical statement: $2/3 < ? < 7/9$
   A) $14/18$
   B) $5/15$
   C) $2/6$
   D) $7/10$

8) A liquid ingredient is stored in 5-quart containers. There are two partially-full containers, one with $4^3/8$ quarts and another with $3^7/8$ quarts. How many quarts are there in total in these two containers?
   A) $1^1/4$
   B) 7
   C) $7^1/8$
   D) $8^1/4$

9) You sell a certain type of liquid cleaner in increments of $1/4$ of a cup. Each 1/4 of a cup costs 50 cents. One customer buys $10^1/4$ cups of this cleaner. How much will she pay for this purchase?
   A) $5.13
   B) $5.50
   C) $10.50
   D) $20.50

10) A customer gives you $160 to pay for the items she purchased, and you gave her the correct change of $12.64. What was the total cost of the items she purchased?
   A) $147.36
   B) $143.76
   C) $137.36
   D) $133.76

11) Your cost of sales figures each month for your first five months of business this year were: $723, $618, $576, $812, and $984. What was the total cost of sales for your first five months of business this year?
   A) $743
   B) $3,623
   C) $3,713
   D) $3,722

12) You had two projects to complete for one particular client this month. You spent $37\frac{2}{5}$ hours on the first project and $25\frac{4}{5}$ hours on the other project. How many hours have you spent on projects for this client this month?
A) $63\frac{1}{5}$
B) $62\frac{1}{5}$
C) $53\frac{1}{5}$
D) $52\frac{1}{5}$

13) For this month, a nurse dispensed 1,275,000 milligrams of medication to patients. How many grams should she report?
A) 127.5
B) 1,275
C) 12,750
D) 1,275,000,000

14) $\frac{1}{8} \div \frac{4}{3} = ?$
A) $\frac{13}{32}$
B) $\frac{32}{3}$
C) $\frac{3}{24}$
D) $\frac{4}{24}$

15) Professor Smith uses a system of extra-credit points for his class. Extra-credit points can be offset against the points lost on an exam due to incorrect responses. David answered 18 questions incorrectly on the exam and lost 36 points. He then earned 25 extra credit points. By how much was his exam score ultimately lowered?
A) −11
B) 11
C) 18
D) 25

16) A group of friends are trying to lose weight. Person A lost $14\frac{3}{4}$ pounds. Person B lost $20\frac{1}{5}$ pounds. Person C lost 36.35 pounds. What is the total weight loss for the group?
A) 70.475
B) 71.30
C) 71.15
D) 71.25

17) Convert the following fraction to decimal format: 5/50
A) 0.0010
B) 0.0100
C) 0.1000
D) 0.0500

18) A job is shared by 4 workers, A, B, C, and D. Worker A does 1/6 of the total hours. Worker B does 1/3 of the total hours. Worker C does 1/6 of the total hours. What fraction represents the remaining hours allocated to person D?
A) $1/8$
B) $3/8$
C) $1/6$
D) $1/3$

19) A furniture store has given a 20 percent discount this month on one of the tables that it sells. This amounts to a discount of $60. What was the original price of the table?
A) $80
B) $120
C) $1200
D) $300

20) A cafeteria is expecting 82 senior citizens for spaghetti this Friday. The spaghetti comes prepared in large containers, and each container holds 15 servings of spaghetti. What is the least number of containers of spaghetti that the cafeteria will need in order to serve all 82 people?
A) 4
B) 5
C) 6
D) 7

21) A caterpillar travels 10.5 inches in 45 seconds. How far will it travel in 6 minutes?
A) 45 inches
B) 63 inches
C) 64 inches
D) 84 inches

22) An ice cream store started the day on Wednesday with $6^3/_4$ quarts of praline nut ice. At the close of business that Wednesday, it had $2^1/_2$ quarts of praline nut ice cream left. How much praline nut ice cream did the store sell that day?
A) $4^1/_4$
B) $4^3/_8$
C) $4^5/_8$
D) $4^6/_8$

23) For one type of decorative stone mix, you have to put in 2 parts of white gravel for every 3 parts of blue slate. You have an order that requires 147 parts of blue slate. How many parts of white gravel should you add?
A) 73.5
B) 88.0
C) 98.0
D) 220.5

24) A small store likes to keep the ratio of bags of apples to bags of oranges at 2 to 3. If there are 44 bags of apples in the store now, how many bags of oranges are there?
A) 66
B) 48
C) 55
D) 33

Algebra and Geometry Problems

25) Simplify the following equation: $(x + 3y)^2$
A) $2(x - 3y)$
B) $2x + 6y$
C) $x^2 + 6xy - 9y^2$
D) $x^2 + 6xy + 9y^2$

26) $(x + 3y)(x - y) = ?$
A) $x^2 + 2xy - 3y^2$
B) $2x + 2xy - 2y$
C) $x^2 - 2xy + 3y^2$
D) $2x - 2y$

27) What is the value of the expression $6x^2 - xy + y^2$ when $x = 5$ and $y = -1$?
   A) 36
   B) 156
   C) 146
   D) 144

28) A circle has a radius of 12. What is the circumference of the circle?
   (Circumference = $\pi \times 2 \times$ radius)
   A) $\pi/12$
   B) $\pi/24$
   C) 24π
   D) 144π

29) Your ceiling is 25 feet wide and 35 feet long. You would like you to use a particular type of square ceiling tile that measures 6 inches by 6 inches. How many of these square ceiling tiles do you need to install this ceiling?
   A) 438
   B) 480
   C) 1,750
   D) 3,500

30) Circle M has a radius of 8, and the area of circle M is 39π greater than the area of circle N. What is the radius of circle N? (area of circle = radius$^2 \times \pi$)
   A) 5π
   B) 5
   C) 6
   D) 6.5

31) You want to enclose a rectangular field that is 12 yards long and 10 yards wide. You are going to use panels, and each panel is 1 yard in length. How many panels are needed in order to enclose the field?
   A) 22
   B) 44
   C) 100
   D) 120

32) Find the volume of a cone which has a radius of 3 and a height of 4.
   Cone volume = ($\pi \times$ radius$^2 \times$ height) ÷ 3
   A) 4π
   B) 12π
   C) $4\pi/3$
   D) $3\pi/4$

8

Look at the diagram below and answer questions 33 to 36

Brooke is going to buy flooring in square pieces that measure 1 square foot each. The entire room is 8 feet by 12 feet. The bookcases are two feet deep from front to back. Flooring will not be put under the bookcases. Each piece of flooring costs $5.50.

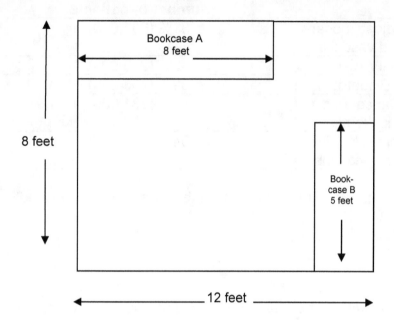

33) What is the area of the floor surface below bookcase A?
A) 8 square feet
B) 16 square feet
C) 20 square feet
D) 64 square feet

34) What is the area of the floor surface below bookcase B?
A) 5 square feet
B) 10 square feet
C) 14 square feet
D) 25 square feet

35) How much will Brooke pay to cover her living room floor?
A) $350   C) $480
B) $385   D) $528

36) If Brooke gets a 27.5% discount off the $5.50 price per tile, how much will she pay to cover her living room floor?
A) $105.88   C) $279.13
B) $253.75   D) $382.80

9

Evaluation of Graphs and Visual Data

Look at the table below and answer questions 37 to 39

Disease or Complication	Percentage of patients with this disease that have survived and total number of patients
Cardiopulmonary and vascular	82% (602,000)
HIV/AIDS	73% (215,000)
Diabetes	89% (793,000)
Cancer and leukemia	48% (231,000)
Premature birth complications	64% (68,000)

37)   Approximately how many patients with diabetes have survived?
A) 58,050
B) 87,230
C) 156,950
D) 705,770

38)   The highest number of deaths occurred as a result of which disease?
A) Cardiovascular and pulmonary disease
B) HIV/AIDS
C) Cancer and leukemia
D) Premature birth complications

39)   The total number of deaths from the two least fatal diseases amounted to which figure below?
A) 82,530
B) 208,960
C) 1,186,040
D) 1,199,410

Look at the graph below and answer questions 40 to 42.

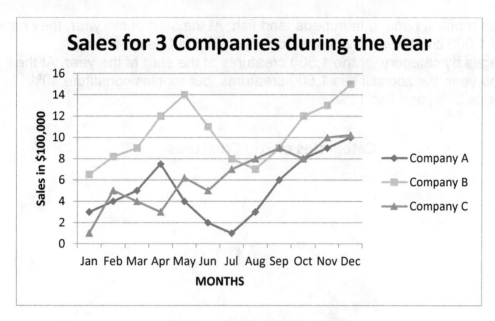

40) Which company had the highest sales figure for July?
A) Company A
B) Company B
C) Company C
D) Companies B and C

41) What was the approximate difference in sales for Company B and Company C in May?
A) Company B's sales were $800,000 more than Company C's.
B) Company C's sales were $800,000 more than Company B's.
C) Company B's sales were $80,000 less than Company C's.
D) Company C's sales were $80,000 less than Company B's.

42) The combined total of sales for all three of the companies was greatest during which month of the year?
A) December
B) November
C) May
D) April

Look at the pie chart and information below and answer questions 43 to 45.

A zoo has reptiles, birds, quadrupeds, and fish. At the start of the year, they have a total of 1,500 creatures living in the zoo. The pie chart below shows percentages by category for the 1,500 creatures at the start of the year. At the end of the year, the zoo still has 1,500 creatures, but reptiles constitute 40%, quadrupeds 21%, and fish 16%.

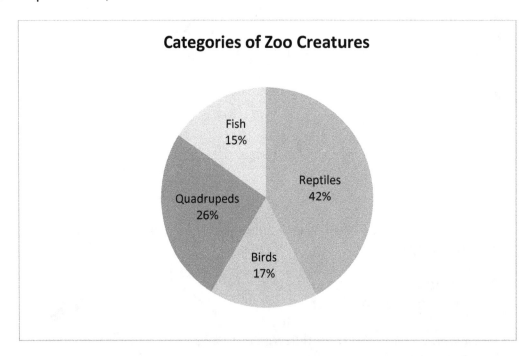

43) How many reptiles are in the zoo at the start of the year?
A) 225
B) 255
C) 390
D) 630

44) What was the difference between the number of quadrupeds at the start of the year and the number of fish at the start of the year?
A) There were 165 more fish than quadrupeds.
B) There were 165 more quadrupeds than fish.
C) There were 75 more fish than quadrupeds.
D) There were 75 more quadrupeds than fish.

45) What can be said about the number of birds at the end of the year when compared to the number of birds at the beginning of the year?
   A) There were 23 more birds at the end of the year than at the beginning of the year.
   B) There were 23 fewer birds at the end of the year than at the beginning of the year.
   C) There were 90 more birds at the end of the year than at the beginning of the year.
   D) There were 90 fewer birds at the end of the year than at the beginning of the year.

WONDERLIC BASIC SKILLS VERBAL PRACTICE TEST 1

For questions 1 to 5, choose the words that best complete the sentence.

1) You would have passed your test _____ more.
   A) had you studied
   B) if you studied
   C) you had studied
   D) would you studied

2) That restaurant has dishes that aren't _____ anywhere else.
   A) to be served
   B) serving
   C) served
   D) to serve

3) _____ it, I can't really say if I like skiing.
   A) Never having tried
   B) Never had trying
   C) Never to have tried
   D) Never to try

4) She would have _____ in the accident had she not put on her seat belt.
   A) injury
   B) been injuring
   C) been injured
   D) to be injured

5) He was evicted from his apartment, but what _____ was pay his rent on time.
   A) he should do
   B) should he do
   C) he should have done
   D) he should be doing

Use the chart below to answer questions 6 to 9.

AMS REF#	Request Date	Description	Action Date	Archive Date
AMS-4987	04/09	Close customer account		
AMS-4988	04/10	Record customer payment	04/18	
AMS-4989	04/08	Issue customer invoice	04/13	06/08
AMS-4990	04/07	Complete customer request	04/12	06/07
AMS-4991	04/06	Update customer record	04/10	06/09
AMS-4992	04/06	Meet with customer	04/08	06/08
AMS-4993	03/30	Assign appointment date	04/03	05/30
AMS-4994	03/29	Send letter to customer	04/02	05/29
AMS-4995	03/28	Assign customer number	04/02	05/28
AMS-4996	03/28	Open customer account	04/01	05/28
AMS-4997	03/27	Make new account request	03/30	05/27
AMS-4998	03/26	Initial customer inquiry	03/31	05/27

6) On what date was AMS-4994 requested?
   A) 03/28
   B) 03/29
   C) 04/02
   D) 05/29

7) Of the completed requests, which one took the fewest days to action?
   A) AMS-4998
   B) AMS-4997
   C) AMS-4996
   D) AMS-4995

8) Of the requests that have been archived, which one had the most days between the request date and archive date?
   A) AMS-4988
   B) AMS-4993
   C) AMS-4992
   D) AMS-4997

9) How many days were there from the request for the initial customer inquiry to the request to close the customer's account?
A) 8
B) 9
C) 13
D) 14

For questions 10 to 13, choose the answer that has the most similar meaning to the underlined word.

10) <u>Acquiesce</u> most nearly means:
A) decide
B) assimilate
C) ignore
D) comply

11) <u>Patent</u> most nearly means:
A) showy
B) obscure
C) visible
D) permitted

12) <u>Lenient</u> most nearly means:
A) easy-going
B) improper
C) lazy
D) insolent

13) <u>Propitiate</u> most nearly means:
A) appease
B) rain
C) modify
D) snow

For questions 14 to 17, choose the word or words that best completes the sentence.

14) Gossiping about others can actually be quite _____ since it can destroy personal reputations.
A) extensive
B) truthful
C) pernicious
D) exciting

15) The house was _____ flames by the time the firefighters arrived.
   A) engulfed in
   B) covered by
   C) ignited with
   D) overcome about

16) He sat by the lake, _____ his problems.
   A) reviewing
   B) contemplating
   C) inspiring
   D) living

17) He was _____ into action after seeing the pictures of the refugees.
   A) treated
   B) fabricated
   C) covered
   D) galvanized

For questions 18 to 21, choose the part of the sentence that contains an error. If the sentence is correct as written, then choose "no error."

18) While both the Black Mountain Poets and the Beat Poets <u>shunned</u> social convention through <u>their</u> experimental art forms, the Black Mountain Poets were affiliated <u>with</u> the Black Mountain College in North Carolina, <u>whereas</u> the Beat Poets were concentrated in California. <u>No error</u>

19) <u>Situated at</u> the site <u>where</u> the Pacific Ocean <u>meets</u> the San Francisco Bay, the Golden Gate <u>spanned</u> by its now-famous bridge, which was completed in 1937. <u>No error</u>

20) <u>Although</u> epiphytes are plants which <u>used</u> other plants for support, they are not parasitic because <u>they</u> have broad leaves that catch water as <u>it</u> drips through the canopy of the tropical forest. <u>No error</u>

21) It is possible <u>to predict</u> when lightening <u>will occur</u> because sparks between clouds and the ground <u>are accompanied</u> by light before <u>it is</u> seen as lightening. <u>No error</u>

17

For questions 22 to 24, read the information below and answer the questions that follow.

SPECIAL INSTRUCTIONS FOR INTERNATIONAL ORDERS

Four large rectangular containers have been placed by the rear door of the shipping room. In the middle of the room, we have placed a special staging station for international orders. All of the packages to be shipped internationally, whether large or small, will be placed in the staging area by the packaging department. Each of these packages must be placed into the appropriate container as follows:

- Container A is for packages that weigh 16 ounces or less.
- Container B for packages with a weight of over 16 ounces, up to 32 ounces.
- Container C is for packages that weigh more than 32 ounces but less than 80 ounces.
- Container D is for all packages that are 80 ounces or more in weight.
- Container E is for all packages that have been damaged. These will be sent back to the packaging department, causing the order to be delayed by 2 days.

If the packages are not sorted correctly, they will not be able to be weighed and will be rejected for shipping. In this case, the shipment of the customer's order will be delayed more than five days. This will very negatively affect our online customer ratings, and we cannot afford for this to happen.

22) According to the instructions, what could cause an order to be delayed more than two days?
A) A package is not sorted correctly by its shape.
B) An 80-ounce package is placed in Container D.
C) A 16-ounce damaged package is placed in Container E.
D) A 32-ounce damaged package is placed in Container B.

23) In which container should an item weighing 80 ounces be placed?
A) Container C
B) Container D
C) Container E
D) Containers C or D

24) According to the information, where is the staging area located?
A) By the rear door
B) By the four large rectangular containers
C) In the middle of the room
D) By the packaging department

18

For questions 25 to 28, read the text below and make any necessary corrections.

(1) A group of English separatists known as the Pilgrims left England to live in Amsterdam in 1608. **(2)** After spending a few years in their new city however many members of the group felt that they did not have enough independence. **(3)** In 1617, the Pilgrims decided to leave Amsterdam to immigrate to America. **(4)** Due to their lack of social standing, they had many financial problems that prevented them from beginning the journey. **(5)** They obtained financing from a well-known London businessman named Thomas Weston, and after 65 days at sea, the Pilgrims reached America, in December, 1620.

25) What change, if any, is needed in sentence 1?
    A) Change separatists to separatists'
    B) Put a comma after the word "Amsterdam"
    C) Change "known as" to "who were"
    D) Make no change

26) What changes, if any, are needed in sentence 2?
    A) Put commas after the word "city" and after the word "however"
    B) Replace the words "did not" with the contraction "didn't"
    C) Place a comma after the word "years"
    D) Make no change

27) Which one of the following words or phrases is best to insert at the beginning of sentence 3?
    A) However,
    B) In addition,
    C) Therefore,
    D) Surprisingly,

28) What change, if any, is needed in sentence 5?
    A) Put the phrase "it was said that" before the word "they"
    B) Change the word "they" to the phrase "the members of the group"
    C) Remove the comma after "America"
    D) Make no change

For questions 29 to 31, choose the sentence that is the most correctly written.

29) A) Non-tariff barriers threaten free trade and limit a country's commerce by impeding its ability to export, to invest, and their financial growth.
     B) Non-tariff barriers threaten free trade and limit a country's commerce by impeding its ability to export, invest, and their financial growth.
     C) Non-tariff barriers threaten free trade and limit a country's commerce by impeding their ability to export, invest, and financial growth.
     D) Non-tariff barriers threaten free trade and limit a country's commerce by impeding its ability to export, to invest, and to grow financially.

30) A) The diplomat mailed the letter to the embassy containing confidential information.
     B) The diplomat mailed the letter containing confidential information to the embassy.
     C) To the embassy, the diplomat mailed the letter containing confidential information.
     D) The diplomat mailed the letter to the embassy, containing confidential information.

31) A) Providing an alternative to other energy sources, nuclear power addresses concerns about increasing air pollution, decreasing fossil fuels, and controlling costs associated with rising inflation.
     B) Providing an alternative to other energy sources, nuclear power addresses concerns about increasing air pollution, decreasing fossil fuels, and helps to control costs associated with rising inflation.
     C) Providing an alternative to other energy sources, nuclear power addresses concerns about increasing air pollution, decreasing fossil fuels, and help to control costs associated with rising inflation.
     D) Providing an alternative to other energy sources, nuclear power addresses concerns about increasing air pollution, decreasing fossil fuels, and to control costs associated with rising inflation.

For questions 32 to 34, choose the group of words that forms a complete sentence.

32) A) To love and be loved for great happiness.
    B) A hot summer day in the middle of July.
    C) Swinging wildly from branch to branch.
    D) The restaurant closes at midnight.

33) A) Fat and skinny and all kinds of people.
    B) Should be finishing then?
    C) The cat who goes from house to house.
    D) Off we go on another adventure!

34) A) Another beautiful day in the neighborhood!
    B) A small puddle under the garage door.
    C) He hopes to start this summer.
    D) Leaving at about 6:00 this evening.

For questions 35 to 37, choose the sentence in which the underlined word has the same meaning as it does in the original sentence.

35) My back began to <u>ache</u> after standing up for such a long time.
    A) She had a dull <u>ache</u> in her back for days after the accident.
    B) If you don't have correct posture, you will get an <u>ache</u> in your neck.
    C) Your feet will <u>ache</u> if your shoes are too small.
    D) Having an <u>ache</u> or pain each day is part of the aging process.

36) The police will <u>comb</u> the site of the incident to look for clues.
    A) You need to <u>comb</u> your hair to make a good impression.
    B) We are going to <u>comb</u> through your things until we find your missing keys.
    C) The <u>comb</u> was on top of the dresser with a brush and mirror.
    D) The rooster had an enormous red <u>comb</u> on the top of its head.

37) We are going to <u>fly</u> to London for vacation next year.
    A) An annoying <u>fly</u> kept buzzing around the house.
    B) You can't just expect to study for your exam on the <u>fly</u>.
    C) The mosquitoes will just <u>fly</u> around us unless we light these candles.
    D) He looked really <u>fly</u> wearing his new sunglasses.

For questions 38 to 40, please refer to the information in the two tables below.

Machine Speeds in Recommended Stitches Per Minute (SPM) **Standard Machine**					
Fabric Weight	Cotton Calico	Rayon	Polyester	Light Denim	Cotton Gingham
Up to $3^3/_8$ oz	750	700	720	870	760
$3^1/_2$ to $4^5/_8$ oz	800	720	730	910	810
$4^3/_4$ to 5 oz	850	740	750	950	860
Over 5 oz	900	760	770	1000	910

Machine Speeds in Recommended Stitches Per Minute (SPM) **Heavy Duty Machine**					
Fabric Weight	Canvas	Heavy Broadcloth	Tapestry Cloth	Medium Denim	Heavy Denim
Up to $3^3/_{16}$ oz	1900	1800	1850	1770	1970
$3^1/_4$ to $5^7/_{16}$ oz	1950	1930	1940	1820	2010
$5^3/_4$ to 7 oz	2000	2010	2030	1880	2030
Over 7 oz	2200	2100	2120	1980	2060

Recommended Needles: #1 = 750 Max SPM; #2 = 900 Max SPM; #3 = 1200 Max SPM; #4 = 2000 Max SPM; #5 = 2200 Max SPM

38) What is the maximum SPM for 3¹/₂-ounce (oz) rayon fabric?
   A) 700
   B) 720
   C) 750
   D) 800

39) An order requires 4-ounce light denim. Which needle will provide the best speed?
   A) 2
   B) 3
   C) 4
   D) 5

40) What needle should be used with 4-ounce tapestry cloth?
   A) 1930
   B) 1940
   C) 3
   D) 4

Go on to the next page.

For questions 41 to 43, read the information below and answer the questions that follow.

Recent research shows that interaction with flowers and other botanicals has many benefits for our health. In fact, several recent studies link floral products with human well-being.

Flower arranging not only combines lovely aromas with beautiful colors and textures, but also makes a person feel closer to nature. In addition, floral design is a creative and calming activity that challenges the mind, requiring its participants to focus on visual skills that improve cognition, information processing, and memory.

Another study found that the mere presence of flowers has an immediate effect on mood and happiness. Those in the study who had frequent contact with an environment that had flowers reported more positive moods and less anxiety. Notably, flowers appeared to have the most positive impact upon seniors, reducing depression and encouraging interaction with others.

These beautiful plants help employees to have more enthusiasm and energy at work as well, leading to innovative thinking and more original solutions. Studies like these seem to confirm what I have always known instinctively: that having flowers makes us feel better in many ways.

41) Why is floral design good for the mind?
   A) It has nice aromas, colors, and textures.
   B) People feel relaxed because they are close to nature.
   C) People have to visualize and think about how to organize the flowers.
   D) It makes its participants happy and in a better mood than before.

42) According to the passage, how is flower arranging good for seniors?
   A) It lessens their anxiety.
   B) It helps them to feel calm.
   C) It makes them feel enthusiastic.
   D) It helps them be more socially active with other people.

43) How does the author feel about flowers?
   A) They are most important for business people.
   B) They can have a positive effect on almost anyone.
   C) Flowers are more beautiful than other botanicals.
   D) Flowers are very beneficial to nature.

For questions 44 to 46, choose the new sentence that joins the original sentences in the best order.

44) The temperature was quite high yesterday.
It really didn't feel that hot outside.
We decided to go out.
A) In spite of the temperature being quite high yesterday, it really didn't feel that hot outside, so we decided to go out.
B) Although we went out yesterday, the temperature was quite high and it really didn't feel hot outside.
C) Even though it didn't feel hot outside, we went outside in spite of the temperature being quite high yesterday.
D) We decided to go out in spite of the temperature being quite high yesterday, and it really didn't feel that hot outside.

45) Our star athlete was in the Olympics.
He had trained for the competition for several years in advance.
He didn't win a gold medal.
A) Despite having trained for the competition for several years in advance, our star athlete didn't receive a gold medal in the Olympics.
B) Our star athlete didn't receive a gold medal, but he had trained for the competition for several years in advance when he went to the Olympics.
C) He had trained for the competition for several years in advance of the Olympics, although our star athlete didn't receive a gold medal.
D) In the Olympics, he didn't receive a gold medal, and our star athlete had trained for the competition for several years.

Go on to the next page.

46) There are acrimonious relationships within our extended family.
Our immediate family decided to go away on vacation during the holiday season.
We wanted to avoid these conflicts.
A) To avoid these conflicts because there are acrimonious relationships within our extended family, our immediate family decided to go away on vacation during the holiday season.
B) Because of acrimonious relationships within our extended family, our immediate family decided to go away on vacation during the holiday season to avoid these conflicts.
C) Due to the fact that there are acrimonious relationships within our extended family, to avoid these conflicts, our immediate family decided to go away on vacation during the holiday season.
D) To avoid these conflicts since our immediate family decided to go away on vacation during the holiday season, there are acrimonious relationships within our extended family.

For questions 47 to 50, choose the word that best indicates the meaning of the underlined word.

47) She is really temperamental in the morning.
A) grumpy
B) alert
C) sleepy
D) energetic

48) The new law will set a(n) precedent.
A) system
B) exemplar
C) regulation
D) authority

49) She was commended for her actions.
A) praised
B) reprimanded
C) reported
D) criticized

50) Ostensibly, he is a nice person.
A) obviously
B) occasionally
C) seemingly
D) rarely

WONDERLIC BASIC SKILLS QUANTITATIVE PRACTICE TEST 2

1) What is the equivalent of 5½ – 2¼?
   A) $3^1/_4$
   B) $3^1/_8$
   C) $3^1/_6$
   D) $3^2/_4$

2) What is the value of 6.55 × 1.2?
   A) 7.68
   B) 7.86
   C) 78.6
   D) 786

3) What is the remainder when 404 is divided by 6?
   A) 2
   B) 3
   C) 4
   D) 0.33

4) What is the value of 99 ÷ 12?
   A) 8.25
   B) 12.12
   C) 0.825
   D) 0.1212

5) What is 1,832 + 791?
   A) 2,632
   B) 2,623
   C) 2,613
   D) 2,523

6) Which of the following is equivalent to $^1/_{16}$?
   A) 0.0625%
   B) 6.25%
   C) 62.5%
   D) 625%

7) A vat contains 163.75 units of red colorant, 107.50 units of blue colorant, 91.25 units of yellow colorant, and 10.30 units of black colorant. Which of the following represents, in terms of units, how full the vat is now?
A) 362.50
B) 371.50
C) 372.80
D) 373.50

8) A new skyscraper is being erected in the city center. The foundation of the building extends 1,135 feet below ground. The building itself, when erected, will measure 13,975 feet above ground. What is the best estimate of the distance between the deepest point below ground and the highest point of the building above ground?
A) 12,000 feet
B) 13,000 feet
C) 14,000 feet
D) 15,000 feet

9) The human resources department has informed you that 4 out of every 5 employee-satisfaction questionnaires have been completed and returned. If your company has 250 total employees, how many questionnaires have not been completed and returned?
A) 4
B) 5
C) 50
D) 200

10) A store sells poinsettia plants for $20 during December and for $12 during January. In December, 55 customers purchased poinsettias, and 20 customers purchased them in January. How much money did the store receive for poinsettia sales during December and January?
A) $240
B) $1,060
C) $1,100
D) $1,340

11) You work as a flight attendant for a major airline. During each flight, you are required to count the number of passengers on board the aircraft. The morning flight had 52 passengers more than the evening flight, and there were 540 passengers in total on the two flights that day. How many passengers were there on the evening flight?
   A) 244
   B) 296
   C) 488
   D) 540

12) A plumber charges $100 per job, plus $25 per hour worked. He is going to do 5 jobs this month. He will earn a total of $4,000. How many hours will he work this month?
   A) 10
   B) 40
   C) 80
   D) 140

13) A restaurant buys soft drink in 20-gallon containers. One container has $19^3/_4$ gallons in it and another has $14^3/_4$ gallons of soft drink. How much soft drink is there in total in these two containers?
   A) 5
   B) $33^1/_2$
   C) $33^3/_4$
   D) $34^1/_2$

14) Mary needs to get $650 in donations. So far, she has obtained 80% of the money she needs. How much money does she still need?
   A) $8.19
   B) $13.00
   C) $32.50
   D) $130.00

15) $^1/_3 - ^1/_7 = ?$
   A) $^1/_{21}$
   B) $^1/_4$
   C) $^3/_7$
   D) $^4/_{21}$

16) Tom bought a shirt on sale for $12. The original price of the shirt was $15. What was the percentage of the discount on the sale?
A) 2%
B) 3%
C) 20%
D) 25%

17) The number of visitors a museum had on Tuesday (T) was twice as much as the number of visitors it had on Monday (M). The number of visitors it had on Wednesday (W) was 20% greater than that on Tuesday. Which equation can be used to calculate the total number of visitors to the museum for the three days?
A) W + .20W + 2T + M
B) 2M + T + W
C) M + 1.2T + W
D) 5.4M

18) You need to install a suspended ceiling for a customer whose ceiling is 25 feet wide and 35 feet long. The customer would like you to use a particular type of square ceiling tile that measures 6 inches by 6 inches. How many of these square ceiling tiles do you need to install this ceiling?
A) 438
B) 480
C) 875
D) 3,500

19) A nurse practitioner in a busy hospital needs to dispense a particular medication in milligrams. However, he needs to fill out the report for the month in grams. For this month, he dispensed 1,275,000 milligrams of medication to patients. How many grams should he report?
A) 127.5
B) 1,275
C) 12,750
D) 127,500,000

20) A dance academy had 300 students at the beginning of January. It lost 5% of its students during the month. However, 15 new students joined the academy on the last day of the month. If this pattern continues for the next two months, how many students will there be at the academy at the end of March?
A) 285
B) 300
C) 310
D) 315

21) You own a store that sells ladies' clothing and accessories. The price of a wool coat is reduced 12.5% at the end of the winter. If the original price of the coat was $120, what will the price be after the reduction?
A) $108.00
B) $107.50
C) $105.70
D) $105.00

22) A factory produces 20 times as many units of Item X as it does Item Y. If the factory produced 11,235 units of Items X and Y in total last week, how many of these units were of Item Y?
A) 535
B) 561
C) 1,070
D) 10,700

23) Which of the following shows the numbers ordered from least to greatest?
A) $-1/4$, $1/8$, $1/6$, 1
B) $-1/4$, $1/8$, 1 , $1/6$
C) $-1/4$, $1/6$, $1/8$, 1
D) $-1/4$, 1 , $1/8$, $1/6$

24) A family buys product A and product B. Product A costs $5 each, and product B costs $8 each. They buy 4 of product A. They also buy a certain quantity of product B. The total value of their purchase is $60. How many units of product B did they buy?
A) 4
B) 5
C) 6
D) 8

25) You can purchase Product A from your supplier for $20 per unit. With your membership card, you can get a $4 discount per unit on Product A from the supplier. Your supplier has started to offer the same percentage discount on Product B. You can normally purchase Product B for $16 per unit. What figure below represents the purchase cost of Product B after the discount?
A) $3.20
B) $4.00
C) $12.00
D) $12.80

26) The term PPM, pulses per minute, is used to determine how many heartbeats an individual has every 60 seconds. In order to calculate PPM, the pulse is taken for ten seconds, represented by variable P. What equation is used to calculate PPM?
A) PPM ÷ 60
B) PPM ÷ 10
C) P6
D) P10

27) The medical authorities have recommended that an individual's ideal PPM is 60. What equation is used to calculate by how much a person's PPM exceeds the ideal PPM?
A) 60 + PPM
B) 60 – PPM
C) PPM + 60
D) PPM – 60

28) You sell socks and shoes in the shoe store that you run. The price of socks is $2 per pair and the price of shoes is $25 per pair. Anna went shopping for socks and shoes, and she paid $85 in total. In this purchase, she bought 3 pairs of shoes. How many pairs of socks did she buy?
A) 2
B) 3
C) 5
D) 8

29) You sell chain-link fence by the $^1/_2$ yard. You sell each $^1/_2$ yard for $10.50. One customer buys $20^1/_2$ yards of this particular type of fence. How much will the customer pay for this purchase?
A) $215.25
B) $225.75
C) $430.50
D) $450.50

30) If $5x - 2(x + 3) = 0$, then x = ?
A) –2
B) –1
C) 1
D) 2

31) A town has recently suffered a flood. The total cost, represented by variable C, which is available to accommodate R number of residents in emergency housing is represented by the equation C = $750R + $2,550. If the town has a total of $55,000 available for emergency housing, what is the greatest number of residents that it can house?
A) 68
B) 69
C) 70
D) 71

32) The perimeter of a rectangle is 350 feet and the width of the shortest side is 75 feet. What is the measurement of the length of the rectangle?
A) 10 feet
B) 90 feet
C) 95 feet
D) 100 feet

Go on to the next page.

33) ABC is an isosceles triangle. Angle DAC is 109° and points A, B, and D are co-linear. What is the measurement of ∠C?

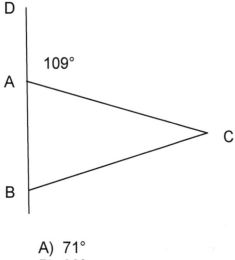

A) 71°
B) 38°
C) 138°
D) 180°

Look at the pie chart below and answer questions 34 to 36.

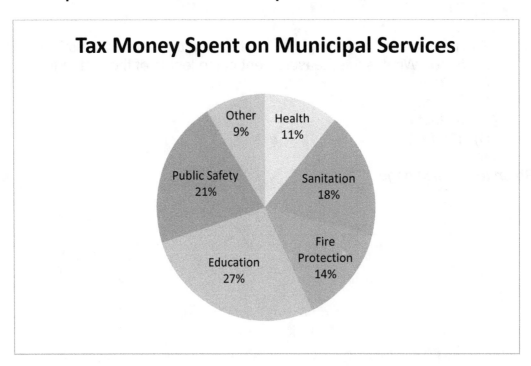

34) According to the chart, the two lowest categories accounted for what percentage of use in total?
   A) 18%
   B) 20%
   C) 23%
   D) 29%

35) If $5,275,300 in total tax money was spend on all municipal services, how much was spent on education?
   A) $474,777
   B) $580,283
   C) $1,107,813
   D) $1,424,331

36) For next year, $6,537,200 in total tax money is budgeted for all municipal services. Each category is allocated the same percentage of next year's budget as the actual percentage spent for the current year. What is the budget amount for public safety?
   A) $915,208
   B) $1,107,813
   C) $1,372,812
   D) $1,765,004

Go on to the next page.

Look at the diagram below and answer questions 37 to 39.

A packaging company secures their packages with plastic strapping prior to shipment. The box is 20 inches in height, 22 inches in depth, and twenty 42 inches in length. For certain packages, 15 extra inches of strapping is used to make a handle on the top of the package to carry it. The strapping is wrapped around the length and width of the entire package, as shown in the following diagram:

37) How many inches of strapping is needed for one package, including making the handle?
A) 124
B) 128
C) 252
D) 267

38) How many inches of strapping is needed to wrap 25 packages if no handles are used?
A) 3,100
B) 3,200
C) 6,300
D) 6,675

39) The volume of the box must be declared prior to shipment. What is the volume in cubic inches of the box shown above?
A) 8,800
B) 16,800
C) 18,480
D) 20,328

Look at the information below and answer questions 40 to 42.

Sam is driving a truck at 70 miles per hour. He will drive through four towns on his route: Brownsville, Dunnstun, Farnam, and Georgetown. At 10:30 am, he sees this sign:

Brownsville	**35 miles**
Dunnstun	**70 miles**
Farnam	**140 miles**
Georgetown	**210 miles**

40) After Sam sees the sign, he continues to drive at the same speed. At 11:00 am, how far will he be from Farnam?
A) He will be in Farnam.
B) He will be 35 miles from Farnam.
C) He will be 70 miles from Farnam.
D) He will be 105 miles from Farnam.

41) Where will Sam be at 12:30 pm?
A) He will be 35 miles past Brownsville.
B) He will be 70 miles from Farnam.
C) He will be 70 miles from Georgetown.
D) He will be 130 miles from Georgetown.

42) What time will Sam arrive in Georgetown if he takes a 30-minute break in Farnam?
A) 1:00 pm
B) 1:30 pm
C) 2:00 pm
D) 2:30 pm

Look at the bar chart below and answer questions 43 to 45.

The chart below shows data on the number of vehicles involved in accidents in Cedar Valley.

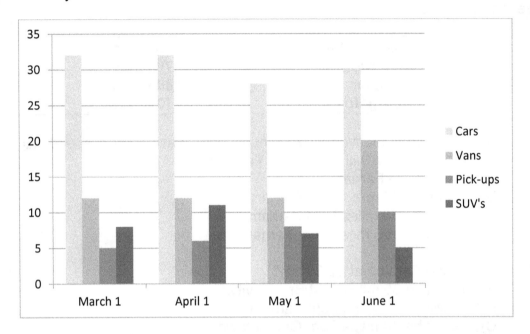

43) Which vehicle accounted for the smallest number of accidents for May 1 and June 1 combined?
   A) Cars   B) Vans   C) Pick-ups   D) SUV's

44) Which vehicle accounted for the largest number of accidents all four dates in total?
   A) Cars   B) Vans   C) Pick-ups   D) SUV's

45) How many accidents involved pick-ups for May 1 and June 1 in total?
   A) 10   B) 11   C) 12   D) 17

WONDERLIC BASIC SKILLS VERBAL PRACTICE TEST 2

For questions 1 to 4, choose the words that best complete the sentence.

1)   The professor was telling us not _____ so much time talking.
         A) spending
         B) to be spending
         C) to spend
         D) be spending

2)   The new fitness center _____ next week.
         A) be opening
         B) is being opening
         C) will opening
         D) is having its opening

3)   Janet told me about the surprise party, although she _____ .
         A) mightn't have
         B) won't have
         C) shouldn't have
         D) couldn't have

4)   I have seen one of Grant Wood's paintings in a museum, but I
         _____ .
         A) from where can't remember
         B) where can't remember
         C) can't remember from where
         D) can't remember where

For questions 5 to 8, choose the answer that has the most similar meaning to the underlined word.

5)   Advocate most nearly means:
         A) judge
         B) adversary
         C) proponent
         D) arbiter

6)   Laud most nearly means:
         A) proclaim
         B) honor
         C) observe
         D) bolster

7) Dubious most nearly means:
    A) unfavorable
    B) undeniable
    C) doubtful
    D) pessimistic

8) Perturb most nearly means:
    A) annoy
    B) fascinate
    C) astound
    D) stimulate

For questions 9 to 11, choose the word that best indicates the meaning of the underlined word.

9) He approaches every task with alacrity.
    A) eagerness
    B) reproach
    C) reluctance
    D) wholesomeness

10) The company has been dormant since 2018.
    A) successful
    B) incorporated
    C) viable
    D) inactive

11) She always has the most ingenious ideas.
    A) benevolent
    B) popular
    C) ridiculous
    D) inventive

For questions 12 to 15, choose the word that best completes the sentence.

12) A(n) _____ gas was being used in order to eliminate the infestation, so we had to leave the building for 24 hours.
   A) invisible
   B) toxic
   C) innocuous
   D) luxurious

13) She was usually _____ about other people's motives and often made cynical comments.
   A) trustworthy
   B) reluctant
   C) skeptical
   D) resisting

14) The judge lessened the sentence for the crime due to _____ circumstances.
   A) extenuating
   B) incriminating
   C) implicating
   D) swindling

15) No one could understand the _____ instructions.
   A) nefarious
   B) expanded
   C) nebulous
   D) completed

Go on to the next page.

For questions 16 to 18, read the information below and answer the questions that follow.

DAY	TOPIC	Max Class 1 Participants	Class 1 Registrations	Max Class 2 Participants	Class 2 Registrations
DAY 1: State-of-the-Art Hardware					
	Platform Differences	1,525	1,287	975	918
	Monitors	1,200	1,098	925	889
	Printers and Scanners	1,375	1,349	965	725
	Other Peripherals	1,485	1,378	950	842
DAY 2: New Developments in Software					
	Operating Systems	1,135	1,056	825	798
	Word Processing	1,350	1,251	815	774
	Data Processing	1,215	1,183	835	776
	Multimedia	1,125	1,074	845	778
DAY 3: The World of Online Technology					
	Internet Search Engines	1,225	1,218	915	889
	Email Interfaces	1,175	1,132	935	912
	RSS Feeds	1,325	1,247	885	823
	Social Media Marketing	1,275	1,255	895	799

16) How many participants are registered for class 2 in data processing?
   A) 835
   B) 774
   C) 776
   D) 1,183

17) Which class has the most registrations, according to the information above?
   A) Social Media Marketing
   B) Other Peripherals
   C) Printers and Scanners
   D) Platform Differences

18) Which class has the smallest number of maximum participants?
   A) Operating Systems
   B) Word Processing
   C) Internet Search Engines
   D) Printers and Scanners

For questions 19 to 21, choose the group of words that forms a complete sentence.

19)   A)   Raining cats and dogs!
      B)   Getting home after 8:00 at night is difficult.
      C)   Cleaning up the attic on Saturday.
      D)   The store going-out-of-business sale.

20)   A)   Try listening for once!
      B)   Offering advice without really heeding it yourself.
      C)   A little problem that could turn into something serious.
      D)   Favorite pets, including cats, rabbits, and hamsters.

21)   A)   Hoping for the best and expecting the worst.
      B)   By the time he is 18, of course.
      C)   A new car would be most useful.
      D)   To give without expectation of anything in return.

For questions 22 to 24, choose the part of the sentence that contains an error. If the sentence is correct as written, then choose "no error."

22)   Originally focusing on suffrage, the <u>Women's</u> Rights Movement expanded

      to include much more <u>than</u> the right to vote and <u>effected</u> the role of women

      in <u>many</u> countries around the world.   <u>No error</u>

23)   The Inca migration <u>from</u> the Peruvian highlands to the area <u>west</u> of the

      Andes <u>constitute</u> an example of the consolidation and extension of the

      <u>tribe's</u> empire in South America.   <u>No error</u>

24)   <u>Ceded by</u> the British <u>to the United States</u> in 1783, the Territory of

      Wisconsin was inhabited by settlers who differed to <u>that</u> of other territories,

      <u>not settling</u> the region in haste as newcomers to other states did.   <u>No error</u>

For questions 25 to 27, read the information below and answer the questions that follow.

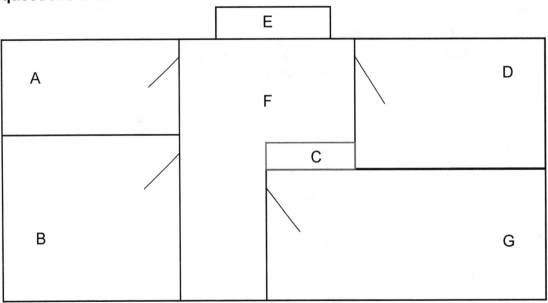

Note: The above drawing is not to scale.

Legend:
A – Storage (4 × 9 feet)
B – Assistant Director's Office (9 × 9 feet)
C – Filing Cabinets
D – Administrative Assistant's Office (7 × 7 feet)
E – Front Door
F – ?
G – Director's Office (7 × 13 feet)

25) The items in the map are listed _____ .
  A) in alphabetical order
  B) at random
  C) for ease of reading
  D) by size

26) These premises would probably be least suitable for which of the following?
  A) A restaurant
  B) A retail business
  C) Commercial offices
  D) Law offices

27) What is most likely the function of area F?
    A) Extra storage
    B) Waiting area with receptionist
    C) Office space for additional worker
    D) Lunch room

For questions 28 to 30, choose the sentence that is the most correctly written.

28) A) Being frustrated and fed up, and tired from a hard week at work, she decided it was time to go away on vacation.
    B) Being frustrated and fed up, and she was tired from a hard week at work, she decided it was time to go away on vacation.
    C) With being frustrated and fed up, and tired from a hard week at work, she decided it was time to go away on vacation.
    D) Frustrated, fed up, and tired from a hard week at work, she decided it was time to go away on vacation.

29) A) Despite the fact he worked overtime several days in a row the congressman didn't finish his report on time.
    B) Despite the fact that he worked overtime several days in a row, the congressman didn't finish his report on time.
    C) In spite of the fact working overtime several days in a row, the congressman didn't finish his report on time.
    D) Although overtime was worked several days in a row, the congressman didn't finish his report on time.

30) A) If text messaging while at the wheel, you could be charged with dangerous driving in some states.
    B) While text messaging at the wheel, you could be charged with dangerous driving in some states.
    C) If you text message while at the wheel, you could be charged with dangerous driving in some states.
    D) If you text messaging while at the wheel, you could be charged with dangerous driving in some states.

45

For questions 31 to 33, read the text below and answer the questions that follow.

Studies of the human body show that performance ability can be enhanced by regular strenuous training exercises. Some human athletic records may seem unbeatable, but these achievements require great effort. When compared to the innate abilities of animals, the athletic training and performance of human beings seem unimpressive, paling in comparison to the phenomenal feats performed naturally by members of the animal kingdom.

Whales, for example, usually dive to 3,700 feet below sea level. However, the human body can withstand underwater depths up to only 2,300 feet, and attempting to do so requires special equipment.

Human performance also seems paltry in swimming when compared to other species. The human record for the fastest swimming speed is 5.3 miles per hour. However, the sailfish averages a speed of 68 miles per hour, and the penguin, which is not even a member of the fish species, can flutter across the surface of the water as fast as 22 miles per hour.

31)   What is the main idea of the passage?
      A) The human body needs training in order to compete in athletic events.
      B) Fish can swim far better than human beings.
      C) Fish can go deeper under water than humans can.
      D) The athletic performance of some animals is superior to that of humans.

32)   According to the passage, why do people sometimes need special diving equipment?
      A) The human body is not designed to cope underwater like fish can.
      B) It is only needed when diving more than 2,300 feet underwater.
      C) It can only be used to depths of up to 3,700 feet.
      D) Because they cannot swim fast enough.

33)   How does the author feel about the athletic performance of animals?
      A) It requires further research.
      B) It is remarkable and extraordinary.
      C) It should be more impressive.
      D) Fish should be able to dive to deeper levels.

For questions 34 to 36, read the text below and answer the questions that follow.

NEW RETURN POLICY

<u>Sporting Goods:</u>
Sporting equipment will continue to be accepted for return as per our previous policy.

However, any items of sportwear or other items of clothing sold in the sporting goods department must now be returned within 7 days from the date of purchase.

The only exception to the above policy change is swimwear, which, as before, cannot be returned in any circumstance as per state health and hygiene laws.

<u>Food and Drink:</u>
We now no longer accept fresh fruit or vegetables for returns, unless they were unfit for human consumption on the date of purchase.

As a result of new laws in our county, we now need to ask for identification from anyone returning alcoholic drinks.

Since we now perform damage checks on merchandise at the point of sale, as of today, we will no longer offer refunds for any item that is damaged.

34) Which item may not be returned in any circumstances?
A) Fresh fruit and vegetables
B) Sporting equipment
C) Sportswear
D) Swimwear

35) Which of the following best reiterates the new damage check policy?
A) No refunds will be offered for damaged items.
B) All merchandise is checked for damage.
C) Damage must be reported within 7 days of purchase.
D) The customer must report damage at the point of sale.

36) A customer wants to return a bikini because she claims that it was torn when she bought it three weeks ago. What should you tell her?
A) Swimwear cannot be returned because of state laws.
B) Swimwear must be returned within 7 days of purchase.
C) She can get a return because swimwear is a sporting good.
D) The store offers refund for damaged goods.

For questions 37 to 41, read the text below and make any necessary corrections.

(1) The most significant characteristic of any population is its age-sex structure, this is defined as the proportion of people of each gender in each different age group. **(2)** The age-sex structures of various populations have social policy implications. **(3)** For instance a population with a high proportion of elderly citizens needs to consider its governmentally-funded pension schemes and health care systems. **(4)** A demographic with a greater percentage of young children should ensure that its educational funding and child welfare policies are implemented efficaciously. **(5)** Low birth rates can also affect the composition of the population, especially if there is a governmental policy that attempts to control demographics by restricting the number of children families' can have.
(6) Demographic change can also occur due to unnaturally high death rates, especially after a disease epidemic or natural disaster has taken place.

37)   What change, if any, is needed in sentence 1?
    A) Change the word "most" to the word "majority"
    B) Change the word "any" to the word "every"
    C) Change the word "this" to the word "which"
    D) Make no change

38)   What change, if any, is needed in sentence 3?
    A) Place a comma after the word "instance"
    B) Change "population" to "populations"
    C) Put a hyphen between "high" and "proportion"
    D) Make no change

39)   Which words, if any, should be added to the beginning of sentence 4?
    A) Just as
    B) Accordingly,
    C) In contrast to
    D) On the other hand,

40) What change, if any, is needed in sentence 5?
   A) Change "rates" to "rate's"
   B) Change "affect" to "effect"
   C) Change "families' " to "families"
   D) Make no change

41) What change, if any, is needed in sentence 6?
   A) Remove the comma after "rates"
   B) Change "has" to "have"
   C) Add a comma after "disaster"
   D) Make no change

For questions 42 to 44, choose the group of words that forms a complete sentence.

42)   A) Just not good for anything is this world.
      B) Staying alert after 11:00 at night is difficult.
      C) Going to see my grandma this weekend.
      D) The college's department of business administration.

43)   A) Eat your meal and be quiet!
      B) Always talking nonstop without listening to others.
      C) Huge stresses in life from all sorts of things.
      D) Eating pizza, cookies, and cake all day long.

44)   A) Praying for a miracle and trying to stay positive.
      B) With a better system that will be installed in the spring.
      C) Lovely though it may seem, vacationing overseas can come with problems.
      D) To keep a business afloat during tough financial times.

For questions 45 to 47, choose the sentence in which the underlined word has the same meaning as it does in the original sentence.

45) Tools and hardware are usually made of <u>iron</u> and other metals.
A) I need to buy an <u>iron</u> and a toaster when I move into my new apartment.
B) Rail lines usually consist of reinforced <u>iron</u> and wooden railway ties.
B) We need to <u>iron</u> out our problems before we can move forward.
C) Having to <u>iron</u> shirts and other items of clothing is such a chore!

46) She is hoping to <u>milk</u> the company for a good settlement for her injury.
A) <u>Milk</u> and other dairy products have really gone up in price lately.
B) He is going to <u>milk</u> that situation for all he can.
C) I am going to learn how to <u>milk</u> a cow when I stay at my aunt's farm.
D) You need to drink <u>milk</u> to get enough calcium in your diet.

47) The <u>matter</u> under consideration is complex and multi-faceted.
A) Scientists are working hard to understand the mysteries of dark <u>matter</u>.
B) The lawyer will look into this legal <u>matter</u> prior to going to court.
C) What is the <u>matter</u> with you today?
D) These mistakes are minor and really don't <u>matter</u>.

For questions 48 to 50, choose the new sentence that joins the original sentences in the best order.

48) My best friend had been feeling extremely sick for several days.
She was stubborn.
She refused to see the doctor.
A) My best friend had been feeling extremely sick for several days, but she was stubborn and refused to see the doctor.
B) My best friend, who was stubborn, had been feeling extremely sick for several days, yet she refused to see the doctor.
C) My best friend had been feeling extremely sick and stubborn for several days, but she refused to see the doctor.
D) My stubborn best friend refused to see the doctor, and had been feeling extremely sick for several days.

49)   He generally doesn't enjoy drinking alcohol.
       He really doesn't like the taste of it.
       He will drink only on social occasions.
       A)   While he generally doesn't enjoy drinking alcohol, he will do so on
            social occasions, and he really doesn't like the taste of it.
       B)   He will drink alcohol on social occasions, but he generally doesn't
            enjoy drinking it and really doesn't like the taste of it.
       C)   Although he generally doesn't enjoy drinking alcohol because he
            doesn't like the taste of it, he will do so on social occasions.
       D)   He really doesn't like the taste of alcohol, but he generally doesn't
            enjoy it, even on social occasions.

50)   The government has made some new policies.
       The policies failed to stimulate spending and expand economic growth.
       The country has slipped further into recession.
       A)   The government's policies failed, in spite of being new, and did not
            stimulate spending and expand economic growth, so the country has
            slipped further into recession.
       B)   The country has slipped further into recession because the policies
            failed to stimulate spending and expand economic growth, which were
            new.
       C)   The government's policies caused the country to slip further into
            recession because they were new and failed to stimulate spending
            and expand economic growth.
       D)   The government's new policies failed to stimulate spending and
            expand economic growth, so the country has slipped further into
            recession.

WONDERLIC BASIC SKILLS QUANTITATIVE PRACTICE TEST 3

1) What is the value of 12 ÷ 80?
   A) 0.015
   B) 0.15
   C) 1.50
   D) 15.0

2) When 1523.48 is divided by 100, which digit of the resulting number is in the tenths place?
   A) 5
   B) 4
   C) 3
   D) 2

3) Which of the following is the least?
   A) 0.028
   B) 0.28
   C) 0.208
   D) 0.82

4) What is the value of 6.83 × 5.2?
   A) 35.516
   B) 35.526
   C) 3.5516
   D) 355.16

5) What is the value of $4^1/_2 - 3^2/_5$?
   A) $^1/_{10}$
   B) $^9/_{10}$
   C) $1^1/_{10}$
   D) $1^9/_{10}$

6) What is 1,832 + 791?
   A) 2,632
   B) 2,623
   C) 2,613
   D) 2,523

7) Which of the following is equivalent to $^1/_{16}$?
   A) 0.0625%
   B) 6.25%
   C) 62.5%
   D) 625%

8) A store received $7,375 for sales of a certain type of scrapbook this year. These scrapbooks were sold for $59 each. How many of them were sold this year?
A) 135
B) 125
C) 120
D) 75

9) $^6/_{25}$ of the inventory has been sold this month. Approximately what percentage of the inventory has been sold?
A) 0.24%
B) 2.40%
C) 24.0%
D) 4.167%

10) Your sales each day for the past five days have been as follows: $90, $85, $85, $105, $110. What was the daily average sales amount during this five-day period?
A) $25
B) $85
C) $90
D) $95

11) You own a fabric store and sell ribbon in 3-inch or one-foot increments. One customer wanted two types of ribbon, and you sold her $8^3/_4$ feet of one type of ribbon and $7^1/_2$ feet of another type. How much ribbon did this customer buy in total?
A) 7 feet and 6 inches
B) 8 feet and 9 inches
C) 15 feet and 3 inches
D) 16 feet and 3 inches

12) Hours spent on a work order for a particular business are recorded by the tenth of an hour in 6-minute increments. For a particular work order, $28^3/_{10}$ hours in total have been budgeted. You have already spent $7^9/_{10}$ hours on the work order. Which amount below represents the amount of time left for this work order?
A) $36^1/_5$
B) $35^6/_{10}$
C) $20^2/_5$
D) $20^3/_5$

13) You manufacture absorbent disposable products that consist of a single layer of absorbent cotton wadding on the inside and a double layer polyvinyl carbonate sheeting on the outside. Each layer of absorbent cotton wadding is 18 inches long, and each layer of polyvinyl carbonate sheeting is 19 inches long. You need to make 18 of these products for a single order. How many feet of materials in total will be required to manufacture this order?
A) 55.5
B) 56
C) 84
D) 666

14) You need $49^3/_{16}$ inches of rope of to finish one job and $18^1/_{16}$ inches to finish another. How many inches of rope do you need in order to complete both jobs?
A) $66^1/_8$
B) $67^1/_8$
C) $66^1/_4$
D) $67^1/_4$

15) When making soda-bread biscuits, the best proportion of baking soda to flour is 2 to 9. You are making a batch of soda-bread biscuits that calls for 126 cups of flour. How many cups of baking soda should you use?
A) 6
B) 7
C) 14
D) 28

16) You worked from 12:10 PM to 2:25 PM knitting 3 caps by hand. At this rate, how many caps will you knit during a 9-hour period?
A) 6
B) 12
C) 36
D) 27

17) Market research shows that 58% of your customers are 10 to 20 pounds overweight and 27% of your customers are 21 to 30 pounds overweight. What percentage below represents the number of customers that are 10 to 30 pounds overweight?
A) 27%
B) 31%
C) 75%
D) 85%

18) You conduct quality control for a factory that makes computer chips. On your most recent shift, you were surprised to discover that 11 out of 132 chips were defective. What percentage best represents the amount of defective computer chips in relation to the total?
A) 0.08%
B) 8%
C) 83%
D) 92%

19) You can buy a case containing 24 bottles of motor oil for $50 a case wholesale. Individual bottles of this brand of motor oil cost $2.50 per bottle wholesale. What is the best price you will pay if you buy 100 bottles of motor oil wholesale?
A) $200.00
B) $200.10
C) $202.50
D) $210.00

20) If $5x - 4(x + 2) = -2$, then $x = $?
A) 8
B) 6
C) -8
D) -6

21) $x^2 + xy - y = 41$ and $x = 5$. What is the value of y?
A) 2.6
B) 4
C) 6
D) -4

22) Mark's final grade for a course is based on the grades from two tests, A and B. Test A counts toward 35% of his final grade. Test B counts toward 65% of his final grade. What equation is used to calculate Mark's final grade for this course?
A) 0.65A + 0.35B
B) 0.35A + 0.65B
C) (0.35A + 0.65B) ÷ 2
D) A + B

23) A runner of a 100-mile endurance race ran at a speed of 5 miles per hour for the first 80 miles of the race and x miles per hour for the last 20 miles of the race. What equation represents the runner's average speed for the entire race?
A) 100 ÷ [(80 ÷ 5) + (20 ÷ x)]
B) 100 × [(80 ÷ 5) + (20 ÷ x)]
C) 100 ÷ [(80 × 5) + (20 × x)]
D) 100 × [(80 × 5) + (20 × x)]

24) What is the value of the expression $2x^2 + 3xy - y^2$ when $x = 3$ and $y = -3$?
A) −18
B) 0
C) 18
D) 36

25) Two people are going to work on a job. The first person will be paid $7.25 per hour. The second person will be paid $10.50 per hour. If A represents the number of hours the first person will work, and B represents the number of hours the second person will work, what equation represents the total cost of the wages for this job?
A) 17.75AB
B) 17.75 ÷ AB
C) AB ÷ 17.75
D) (7.25A + 10.50B)

26) A rectangle has a length of 18 inches and a width of 10 inches. What is the perimeter of the rectangle in inches?
A) 36
B) 46
C) 56
D) 180

27) The perimeter of a rectangle is 350 feet and the width is 75 feet. What is the measurement of the length of the rectangle?
A) 10 feet
B) 90 feet
C) 95 feet
D) 100 feet

28) The radius (R) of circle A is 5 centimeters. The radius of circle B is 3 centimeters. Which of the following statements is true? (Use 3.14 for π)
A) The difference between the areas of the circles is approximately 6.28.
B) The difference between the areas of the circles is approximately 28.26.
C) The difference between the circumferences of the circles is approximately 6.28.
D) The difference between the circumferences of the circles is approximately 12.56.

29) A rectangular box has a base that is 5 inches wide and 6 inches long. The height of the box is 10 inches. What is the volume of the box in cubic inches? (Box volume = L × W × H)
A) 30
B) 110
C) 150
D) 300

30) Find the approximate volume of a cone which has a radius of 3 and a height of 4.
A) 12.56
B) 37.68
C) 4.1762
D) 2.355

31) Pat wants to put wooden trim around the floor of her family room. Each piece of wood is 1 foot in length. The room is rectangular and is 12 feet long and 10 feet wide. How many pieces of wood does Pat need for the entire perimeter of the room?
A) 22
B) 44
C) 100
D) 120

Look at the bar chart below and answer questions 32 to 34.

An athlete ran 10 miles in 1.5 hours. The graph below shows the miles the athlete ran every 10 minutes.

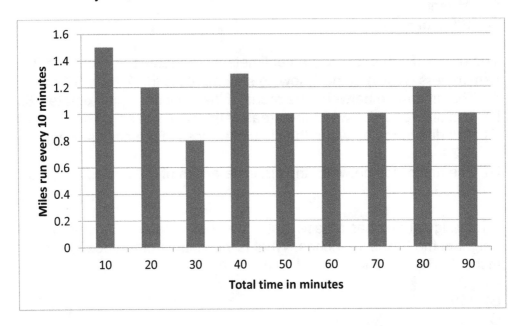

32) What was the most common distance per 10-minute interval?
A) 0.8 mile
B) 1 mile
C) 1.2 miles
D) 1.3 miles

33) What was the difference between the best distance and the worst distance for the data provided above?
A) 0.7 mile
B) 0.8 mile
C) 1 mile
D) 1.2 miles

34) Which figure best represents the average time per 10-minute interval?
A) 9 minutes
B) 10 minutes
C) 0.9 minute
D) 1 minute

Look at the diagram and information below and answer questions 35 to 37.

Each square in the diagram below is one yard wide and one yard long. The gray area of the diagram represents New Town's water reservoir. The white area represents the surrounding conservation park.

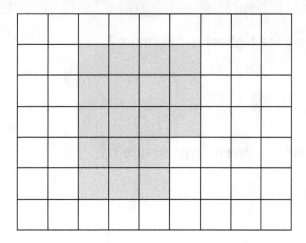

35) What is the perimeter in yards of the reservoir?
A) 18
B) 28
C) 32
D) 63

36) What is the area in square yards of the surrounding conservation park?
A) 18
B) 44
C) 45
D) 46

37) Which of the following ratios represents the area of the reservoir to the area of the surrounding conservation park?
A) 2:5
B) 9:23
C) 17:32
D) 18:44

Look at the table below and answer questions 38 to 41.

Sunday	Monday	Tuesday	Wednesday	Thursday	Friday	Saturday
–10°F	–9°F	1°F	6°F	8°F	13°F	12°F

38) Which day had the highest temperature?
A) Friday
B) Saturday
C) Sunday
D) Monday

39) Which day had the lowest temperature?
A) Friday
B) Saturday
C) Sunday
D) Monday

40) What was the high temperature minus the low temperature?
A) 22
B) –22
C) 23
D) –23

41) What was the average temperature for the week?
A) 1°
B) 3°
C) 6°
D) 22°

Look at the information below and answer questions 42 to 45.

Chantelle took a test that had four parts. The total number of questions on each part is given in the table below, as is the number of questions that Chantelle answered correctly.

Part	Total Number of Questions	Number of Questions Answered Correctly
1	15	12
2	25	20
3	35	32
4	45	32

42) How many points did Chantelle score on the entire exam?
   A) 92
   B) 94
   C) 96
   D) 98

43) How many points in total were there on parts 3 and 4 of the test?
   A) 60
   B) 64
   C) 70
   D) 80

44) Which fraction below best represents the relationship of Chantelle's incorrect answers on Part 1 to the total points on Part 1?
   A) 1/5
   B) 1/3
   C) 4/5
   D) 4/6

45) What was Chantelle's percentage score of correct answers for the entire test?
   A) 75%
   B) 80%
   C) 86%
   D) 90%

WONDERLIC BASIC SKILLS VERBAL PRACTICE TEST 3

For questions 1 to 4, choose the words that best complete the sentence.

1)   That presentation was far too advanced _____ as an introductory lecture.
A) to be suiting
B) for suiting
C) to be suitable
D) suitably

2)   He is _____ his three brothers.
A) taller of
B) the tallest
C) taller than
D) tallest of

3)   We couldn't have completed the project without Ahmed, who _____ a great deal of expertise to the team.
A) brought
B) had brought
C) will have brought
D) will be bringing

4)   Once he _____ that he wasn't going to be able to go to college, he felt a lot better.
A) accepts
B) did accept
C) will accept
D) had accepted

For questions 5 to 8, choose the answer that has the most similar meaning to the underlined word.

5)   <u>Servility</u> most nearly means:
A) hospitality
B) abandonment
C) hostility
D) submissiveness

6) <u>Indispensable</u> most nearly means:
A) permanent
B) superfluous
C) necessary
D) non-degradable

7) <u>Sycophant</u> most nearly means:
A) musician
B) flatterer
C) complainer
D) superior

8) <u>Upheaval</u> most nearly means:
A) movement
B) launch
C) tumult
D) hoist

For questions 9 to 12, choose the word that best completes the sentence.

9) The suspect was _____ for the crime.
A) charged
B) exonerated
C) deliberated
D) relieved

10) Since she often wears vintage and recycled garments, people say that her taste in clothing is very _____.
A) unconventional
B) traditional
C) modern
D) stingy

11) Their troubled relationship is full of _____.
A) sarcasm
B) ambiguity
C) acrimony
D) irony

12) Carrying out their complex strategy involved _____ planning.
A) intricate
B) manageable
C) fortuitous
D) cooperative

For questions 13 to 15, read the information below and answer the questions that follow.

13) Which section in Part 2 is most likely to include the most information on the keyboard and mouse?
   A) Platform Differences
   B) Monitors
   C) Printers and Scanners
   D) Other Peripherals

14) Which part of the book is most likely to address the care and maintenance of computer equipment?
   A) Part 1
   B) Part 2
   C) Part 3
   D) Part 4

15) Where can the reader find the names of the people and organizations that the author has thanked for their support during the writing of the book?
A) Acknowledgments
B) Recommendations
C) Bibliography
D) Index

For questions 16 to 18, read the text below and answer the questions that follow.

Working in a run-down laboratory near Paris, Marie Curie worked around the clock to discover a radioactive element. When she finally captured her quarry in 1902, she named it "radium" after the Latin word meaning ray.

Madame Curie should certainly be an inspiration to scientists today. She had spent the day blending chemical compounds which could be used to destroy unhealthy cells in the body. As she was about to retire to bed that evening, she decided to return to her lab. There she found that the chemical compound had become crystalized in the bowls and was emitting the elusive light that she sought.

Inspired by the French scientist Henri Becquerel, Curie won the Nobel Prize for Chemistry in 1903. Upon winning the prize, she declared that the radioactive element would be used only to treat disease and would not be used for commercial profit.

Today radium provides an effective remedy for certain types of cancer. Radium, now used for a treatment called radiotherapy, works by inundating diseased cells with radioactive particles. Its success lies in the fact that it eradicates malignant cells without any lasting ill effects on the body.

16) According to the information in the passage, why is radium treatment used as a cancer therapy?
A) because it is cost effective
B) because it destroys cancerous cells
C) because it has no long-term effects
D) because it derives from a radioactive element

17) What is the most appropriate title of the passage?
A) The Discoveries of Madame Curie
B) The Use of Radium to Treat Cancer
C) Madame Curie: A Brief Biography
D) The Discovery and Use of Radium

18) Which of the following phrases or sentences from the passage expresses an opinion rather than a fact?
   A) Marie Curie worked around the clock to discover a radioactive element.
   B) Madame Curie should certainly be an inspiration to scientists today.
   C) She had spent the day blending chemical compounds which could be used to destroy unhealthy cells in the body.
   D) Upon winning the prize, she declared that the radioactive element would be used only to treat disease and would not be used for commercial profit.

For questions 19 to 22, choose the part of the sentence that contains an error. If the sentence is correct as written, then choose "no error."

19) It is difficult <u>to know</u> <u>when</u> people first began to grow sweet potatoes, <u>because</u> early settlers often did not differentiate this vegetable <u>from</u> other tubers. <u>No error</u>

20) Commencing in 1847 and for <u>nearly</u> 16 years <u>thereafter</u>, Mexico City was occupied by U.S. troops until it <u>had been</u> conquered by Maximilian, a ruler whose name <u>originates from</u> the Roman word *maximus*. <u>No error</u>

21) Scientists <u>have discovered</u> that most comets that orbit around the sun <u>seems</u> to <u>be composed</u> of rock and dust particles embedded in ice. <u>No error</u>

22) <u>Even though</u> chicory is usually cooked, <u>their</u> leaves <u>can be eaten</u> in various ways, including as a raw ingredient in salads or <u>as a dried</u> and ground substitute for coffee. <u>No error</u>

For questions 23 to 25, choose the sentence that is the most correctly written.

23) A) Drafting the *Declaration of Independence*, and he served as Secretary of State, Thomas Jefferson has a prominent place in US history.
B) By drafting the *Declaration of Independence*, and he served as Secretary of State, Thomas Jefferson has a prominent place in US history.
C) Drafting the *Declaration of Independence* and serving as Secretary of State, Thomas Jefferson has a prominent place in US history.
D) Drafting the *Declaration of Independence* and to serve as Secretary of State, Thomas Jefferson has a prominent place in US history.

24) A) Honeysuckle is a well-known species of climbing plant native to the northern hemisphere and often grown consequently for ornamental purposes in patios and gardens.
B) Honeysuckle, a well-known species of climbing plant native to the northern hemisphere, and thus is often grown for ornamental purposes in patios and gardens.
C) Honeysuckle is a well-known species of climbing plant native to the northern hemisphere and furthermore often grown for ornamental purposes in patios and gardens.
D) Since honeysuckle is a well-known species of climbing plant native to the northern hemisphere, it is often grown for ornamental purposes in patios and gardens.

25) A) Overworked and underpaid many employees seek help from their union representatives.
B) Overworked and underpaid, many employees seeking help from their union representatives
C) Overworked and underpaid, many employees seek help from their union representatives
D) Many overworked and underpaid employees seek, help from their union representatives

For questions 26 to 28, read the information below and answer the questions that follow.

Any club member who holds an Elite Status Card will now get discounts off the price of guest admissions, in addition to the other rewards and perks of the Elite Status program. Please follow the guidelines given below:

Guest admissions for meals
- The member must accompany his or her guest for a meal.
- If the member does not show an Elite Status Card, please ask him or her to do so.
- Note down the price of the guest's food and drink on the Guest Discount for Meals ticket.
- Write your signature and the date on the 10% Guest Discount for Meals Ticket and place it in the accounting department in-box.
- The meal discount can be offered only between 11 am and 11 pm.

Guest admissions for the spa
- The member must accompany his or her guest for a spa treatment.
- If the member does not show an Elite Status Card, please ask him or her to do so.
- Use the cash register to take 20% off the price of the guest's spa treatment.
- Initial the receipt.
- The spa discount can only be offered when the spa is open.

26) You work in the restaurant. What should you write on the appropriate ticket?
   A) 10% off
   B) Guest discount for meals
   C) Your signature and the date
   D) Accounting department

27) In order to receive admission to the spa, a guest should:
   A) show an Elite Status Card.
   B) be accompanied by a member.
   C) initial their receipt.
   D) arrive between 11 am and 11 pm.

28) Which of the following best describes how the Elite Status Card may be used?
   A) The card may be loaned to guests.
   B) The card is used only to receive discounts.
   C) The card must have a signature.
   D) The card confers various benefits to members and their guests,

For questions 29 to 31, choose the group of words that forms a complete sentence.

29) A) Before we even realized or understood it.
   B) Away we go to grandmother's house!
   C) Looking intelligent and sophisticated with his glasses on.
   D) The last chance before they move to Denver.

30) A) The old, the new, the borrowed, and the blue are all here.
   B) Studying while working a full-time job.
   C) Shouldn't cost the earth, should it?
   D) A cow grazing peacefully in the field.

31) A) Time and time again without fail!
   B) The summertime concerts at 5:00 in the park.
   C) Talking without listening can lead to misunderstandings.
   D) Gently giving way in the gentle spring wind.

Go on to the next page.

For questions 32 to 37, read the text below and make any necessary corrections.

(1) Organic farming and organic produce create many positive outcomes for the environment. **(2)** However, did you know that most mainstream American consumers have reservations about organic food. **(3)** The first drawback that consumers perceive is the cost of course. **(4)** Consumers with higher income levels can afford organically-grown food, but many people simply do not believe that these are worth the added expense. **(5)** There are also issues about the safety of organic food due to using cow manure and the use of other animal waste as fertilizer. **(6)** Take the case of windfall apples, which are apples that fall off the tree, these apples can be contaminated by the cow manure. **(7)** This contamination occurs because manure contains a virulant bacterium known as known as e-coli. **(8)** Because of these concerns, it may be quite some time before the purchase of organic food became the norm in American households.

32) What change, if any, is needed in sentences 1 and 2?
    A) Change "produce" to "product"
    B) Change "outcomes" to "out comes"
    C) Change the second period to a question mark.
    D) Make no change

33) What change, if any, is needed in sentence 3?
    A) Add a comma after "cost"
    B) Change "perceive" to "percieve"
    C) Change "is" to "was"
    D) Make no change

34) What change, if any, is needed in sentence 4?
    A) Remove the comma after "food"
    B) Change "simply" to "simple"
    C) Change "these are" to "it is"
    D) Make no change

35) What change, is any, is needed in sentence 5?
A) Change "concerns" to "concern"
B) Delete the phrase "the use of"
C) Change "fertilizer" to "fertalizer"
D) Make no change

36) What change, if any, is needed in sentence 6?
A) Change the second comma to a period and capitalize "these"
B) Add the words "If you" before "Take"
C) Change "which" to "that"
D) Make no change

37) What change, if any, is needed in sentence 7?
A) Change "occurs" to "occur"
B) Change "virulent" to "virulent"
C) Change "as" to "is"
D) Make no change

For questions 38 to 40, choose the sentence in which the underlined word has the same meaning as it does in the original sentence.

38) We need to be able to <u>trust</u> one another in this relationship.
A) All of the money was being held in <u>trust</u>.
B) I would <u>trust</u> him with my life.
C) The <u>trust</u> between us has died after she betrayed me so badly.
D) Access to the <u>trust</u> fund will be granted when he turns 18.

39) All of the students were <u>present</u> for the group assembly.
A) I got a really nice <u>present</u> from my parents for my birthday.
B) The chairperson will <u>present</u> you with the award at the ceremony.
C) You need to count how my members are absent, as well as how many are <u>present</u>.
D) At the <u>present</u> moment, I don't have an opinion on this issue.

40) The soldier will <u>report</u> for duty when called by the superior officer.
A) The financial <u>report</u> stated the income and expenses of the company.
B) There was a <u>report</u> about an accident on the radio this morning.
C) The shotgun has a very loud <u>report</u> when it is fired.
D) I need to <u>report</u> for work at 9:00 AM on Saturday.

For questions 41 to 43, choose the new sentence that joins the original sentences in the best order.

41) Students may need prerequisites for some classes.
Students may attend other classes without fulfilling a prerequisite.
However, students are advised that non-required introductory classes are beneficial.
   A) Students are advised of the benefit of non-required introductory courses, although they may attend their classes without fulfilling prerequisites.
   B) Even though students may attend certain classes without fulfilling a prerequisite, they are advised of the benefit of non-required introductory courses.
   C) While students are advised of the benefit of non-required introductory courses, some classes need a prerequisite, but others don't need this.
   D) Even though they may attend some classes by fulfilling a prerequisite, students are advised of the benefit of non-required introductory courses, but this doesn't apply to all classes.

42) There have been advances in technology.
Medical science has also improved recently.
Because of this, infant mortality rates have declined substantially in recent years.
   A) Owing to advances in technology and medical science, infant mortality rates have declined substantially in recent years.
   B) Since infant mortality rates have declined substantially in recent years, there have been advances in technology and medical science.
   C) While infant mortality rates have declined substantially in recent years, there have been improvements in technology and medical science has also advanced.
   D) There have been improvements in technology and medical science has also advanced, leading to infant mortality rates declining substantially in recent years.

43) It was the most expensive restaurant in town.
It provided the worst service.
The staff was also rude to customers.
   A) It was the most expensive restaurant in town, besides having rude staff and providing the worst service.
   B) In addition to being the most expensive restaurant in town, it had rude staff because it provided the worst service.
   C) The expensive restaurant had rude, terrible servers.
   D) Although having rude staff and providing the worst service, it was the most expensive restaurant in town

72

For questions 44 to 46, read the text below and answer the questions that follow.

Recent studies show that coffee may be even worse for us than we thought. We have known for a few years now that coffee can elevate blood pressure and also lead to high cholesterol, but new research has revealed a whole host of other health problems caused by the beverage. A new study demonstrates that coffee stimulates the secretion of gastric acid, which can lead to stomach upset. So, if you frequently suffer from stomach ache, it would be a good idea to cut down on coffee or stop drinking it altogether.

Consuming coffee later in the day is strongly linked to insomnia, which can cause health problems like anxiety and depression. Caffeine stays in your system for six hours, so don't have coffee after 2:00 pm unless you drink decaffeinated.

A further study has shown that coffee changes our sense of taste, making sweet things seem less sweet. This may cause us to crave more sweets. However, avoid adding sugar, cream, or milk to your coffee. With raised calorie levels, continued consumption of such sugar-laden beverages can lead to obesity and type-two diabetes.

44) What does the author mention about high cholesterol?
     A) It leads to gastric acid.
     B) It can be caused by drinking coffee.
     C) It results only from drinking coffee.
     D) It is linked to high blood pressure.

45) According to the passage, how can coffee cause stomach ache?
     A) Drinking too much of it fills up the stomach.
     B) The caffeine in the beverage irritates the stomach.
     C) It makes acidity levels in the stomach higher.
     D) Stomach ache is linked to adding too much sugar.

46) Why does the author mention anxiety and depression?
     A) to exemplify another problem caused by drinking too much coffee
     B) to demonstrate that caffeine remains in the human body for several hours
     C) to illustrate how caffeine is related to insomnia
     D) to criticize coffee drinkers for overindulging in the beverage

For questions 47 to 50, choose the word that best indicates the meaning of the underlined word.

47) The governor decided to show <u>clemency</u> to the prisoners.
A) justice
B) peace
C) mercy
D) hope

48) He said that we have to <u>abridge</u> the document.
A) shorten
B) mail
C) interpret
D) file

49) Of all of the volunteers on the campaign, she has been the most <u>stalwart</u>.
A) dependable
B) defensive
C) compromising
D) submissive

50) The high salary <u>enticed</u> him into accepting the job.
A) tricked
B) lured
C) blackmailed
D) bribed

WONDERLIC BASIC SKILLS QUANTITATIVE PRACTICE TEST 4

1) $- (-5) + 3 = ?$
   A) -8
   B) -2
   C) 2
   D) 8

2) Estimate the result of the following: $502 \div 49.1$
   A) 8
   B) 9
   C) 10
   D) 11

3) What is $^1/_3 \times {}^2/_3$?
   A) $^2/_3$
   B) $^2/_6$
   C) $^2/_9$
   D) $^1/_3$

4) Simplify: $\dfrac{12}{27}$

   A) $\dfrac{1}{3}$

   B) $\dfrac{3}{4}$

   C) $\dfrac{3}{9}$

   D) $\dfrac{4}{9}$

5) $3\frac{1}{2} - 2\frac{1}{3} = ?$

A) $\dfrac{1}{3}$

B) $\dfrac{9}{3}$

C) $\dfrac{5}{6}$

D) $1\frac{1}{6}$

6) A hockey team had 50 games this season and lost 20 percent of them. How many games did the team win?
A) 8
B) 40
C) 20
D) 10

7) Carmen wanted to find the average of the five tests she has taken this semester. She erroneously divided the total points from the five tests by 4, which gave her a result of 90. What is the correct average of her five tests?
A) 72
B) 80
C) 64
D) 90

8) In a high school, 17 out of every 20 students participate in a sport. If there are 800 students at the high school, what is the total number of students that participate in a sport?
A) 120 students
B) 640 students
C) 680 students
D) 776 students

9) In a particular class, 2 in 25 students get straight A's. What percentage best represents the number of straight-A students in this class?
A) 0.08%
B) 8%
C) 83%
D) 92%

10) A liquid solution needs 2 ounces of Chemical F for every 7 ounces of Chemical G. You are making a batch of the solution that requires 147 ounces of Chemical G. How many ounces of Chemical F should you add?
A) 42
B) 24
C) 21
D) 49

11) You worked from 1:10 AM to 3:25 AM making 3 units of Item X. At this rate, how many units of item X will you make during a 9-hour period?
A) 6
B) 12
C) 36
D) 27

12) Research shows that 29% of your clients have from $0 to $5,000 in disposable income a month and 17% of your clients have from $5,001 to $10,000 in disposable income a month. What percentage below represents the number of clients that have from $0 to $10,000 in disposable income a month?
A) 12%
B) 36%
C) 46%
D) 17%

13) In a math class, $1/3$ of the students fail a test. If twelve students have failed the test, how many students are in the class in total?
A) 15
B) 16
C) 36
D) 38

14) Yesterday a train traveled $117^3/_4$ miles. Today it traveled $102^1/_6$ miles. What is the difference between the distance traveled today and yesterday?
A) 15 miles
B) $15^1/_4$ miles
C) $15^7/_{12}$ miles
D) $15^9/_{12}$ miles

15) Kathy is on a diet. During week 1, she lost 1.07 pounds. During week 2, she lost 2.46 pounds. During week 3, she lost 3.92 pounds. If each week's weight loss amount is rounded up or down to the nearest one-tenth of a pound, what is the estimate of Kathy's weight loss for the entire 3 weeks?
A) 7 pounds
B) 7.40 pounds
C) 7.45 pounds
D) 7.50 pounds

16) Sandra needs to calculate 16% of 825. Which of the following formulas can she use?
A) 825 × 16
B) 16 × 825
C) 825 × 16
D) 825 × 0.16

17) Wayne bought a shirt on sale. The original price of the shirt was $18, and he got a 40% discount. What was the sales price of the shirt?
A) $7.20
B) $10.80
C) $11.80
D) $17.28

18) You need to have at least 50 quarts of PVA in stock at the start of every month. You have taken inventory this morning and have found that you have 2 containers of PVA that hold 16 cups and 7 ounces each. You also have 3 containers of PVA that hold 20 cups and 4 ounces each. You must purchase this PVA in 5-quart containers. How many containers do you need to buy in order to replenish your stock?
A) 0
B) 5
C) 6
D) 7

19) Parabens are stored in two identically sized vats. The vats measure 10 feet by 10 feet by 12 feet. The first vat is $3/4$ full and the second vat is $4/5$ full. The parabens cost 12 cents a cubic inch. To the nearest dollar, what is the cost value of the parabens in the two vats?
A) $223
B) $3,857
C) $4,977
D) $385,690

20) You worked 7.5 hours each day for 2 days on a job for one customer. The customer was billed $75 per hour for your work, and you were paid $40 per hour. How much money did the shop make for your work on this job after paying your wages?
A) $262.50
B) $300.00
C) $525.00
D) $600.00

21) You have a liquid ingredient that you store in 5-quart containers. You have two partially-full containers, one with $4^3/_8$ quarts and another with $3^7/_8$ quarts. How many quarts do you have in total in these two containers?
A) $1^1/_4$
B) 7
C) $7^1/_8$
D) $8^1/_4$

22) According to your measurements, you started the day with $12^7/_{16}$ yards of tarpaulin. When you take measurements again at the end of the day, you have $8^9/_{16}$ yards of tarpaulin left. Which amount below represents the amount of tarpaulin used this day in yards?
A) $2^{14}/_{16}$
B) $3^1/_8$
C) $3^7/_8$
D) $4^7/_8$

23) You have purchased 80 items for sale and have sold 0.75 of them in relation to the total purchased. How many items do you have left after making these sales?
A) 10 items
B) 20 items
C) 25 items
D) 40 items

24) The temperature on Saturday was 62°F at 5:00 PM and 38°F at 11:00 PM. If the temperature fell at a constant rate on Saturday, what was the temperature at 9:00 PM?
A) 58°F
B) 54°F
C) 50°F
D) 46°F

25) You can buy cotton cloth for your textile manufacturing company for $3 a meter from an overseas supplier. However, you need to report the cost of the cloth in inches for your financial statements for the board of directors. How many inches of cloth can you get for $3?
A) 2.54
B) 3.937
C) 39.37
D) 100

26) Mrs. Johnson is going to give candy to the students in her class. The first bag of candy that she has contains 43 pieces. The second contains 28 pieces, and the third contains 31 pieces. If there are 34 students in Mrs. Johnson's class, and the candy is divided equally among all of the students, how many pieces of candy will each student receive?
A) 3 pieces
B) 4 pieces
C) 5 pieces
D) 51 pieces

27) A city wants to build a new library. The total cost of the project is represented by variable L, calculated by charging $250 per square foot. A down payment of $30,000 needs to be paid upfront. If the total cost of the project is $281,250, what is the approximate size in square feet of the library?
A) 1125
B) 1135
C) 1005
D) 1015

28) In a particular class, $t\%$ of the students subscribe to digital TV packages. Which of the following represents the number of students who do not subscribe to any digital TV package?
A) $100(n - t)$
B) $(100\% - t\%) \times n$
C) $(100\% - t\%) \div n$
D) $(1 - t)n$

29) $x^2 + xy - y = 254$ and $x = 12$. What is the value of y?
A) 110
B) 10
C) 11
D) 12

30) $(3x + y)(x - 5y) = ?$
   A) $3x^2 - 14xy - 5y^2$
   B) $3x^2 - 14xy + 5y^2$
   C) $3x^2 + 14xy - 5y^2$
   D) $3x^2 + 14xy + 5y^2$

31) Factor: $9x^3 - 3x$
   A) $3x(3x^2 - 1)$
   B) $3x(3x - 1)$
   C) $3x(x^2 - 1)$
   D) $3x(x - 3)$

32) The price of a sofa at a local furniture store was x dollars on Wednesday this week. On Thursday, the price of the sofa was reduced by 10% of Wednesday's price. On Friday, the price of the sofa was reduced again by 15% of Thursday's price. Which of the following expressions can be used to calculate the price of the sofa on Friday?
   A) $(0.75)x$
   B) $(0.10)(0.15)x$
   C) $(0.10)(0.85)x$
   D) $(0.90)(0.85)x$

33) You are preparing a drawing that contains a triangle. The triangle has one angle, labeled Angle A, which measures 36°. You are missing the measurements for angles B and C of this triangle. However, you have noted that angles B and C have the same measurement each in degrees. What is the measurement of angle B?
   A) 36°
   B) 45°
   C) 72°
   D) 144°

34) A living room is 25 feet long and 10 feet wide. A light will be installed on each wall in 5-foot increments. However, no lights are to be installed in the corners of the room. How many lights will you need to carry out this job?
   A) 8
   B) 10
   C) 12
   D) 14

35) A farmer has a small pasture that has a length of 5 yards and a width of 3 yards. Barbed wire must be placed on all four sides of the outside of this pasture. How many yards of barbed wire should he order?
A) 15
B) 16
C) 18
D) 40

36) If circle A has a radius of 0.4 and circle B has a radius of 0.2, what is the difference in area between the two circles? (Use 3.14 for π)
A) 0.1256
B) 0.3768
C) 0.5024
D) 1.256

37) Find the area of the right triangle that has a base of 4 and a height of 15. (Triangle area = base × height ÷ 2)
A) 20
B) 30
C) 60
D) 12

38) The triangle in the illustration below is an equilateral triangle, which has three equal angles. What is the measurement in degrees of angle *a*?

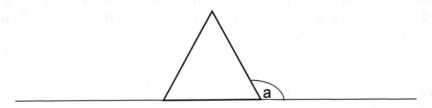

A) 45
B) 60
C) 120
D) 180

39)   The radius (R) of circle A is 5 centimeters. The radius of circle B is 3 centimeters. Which of the following statements is true?

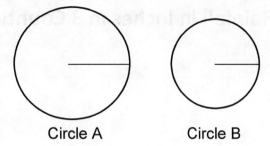

Circle A   Circle B

A) The difference between the areas of the circles is 2.
B) The difference between the areas of the circles is 9π.
C) The difference between the circumferences of the circles is 2.
D) The difference between the circumferences of the circles is 4π.

Go on the next page.

Look at the bar chart below and answer questions 40 to 42.

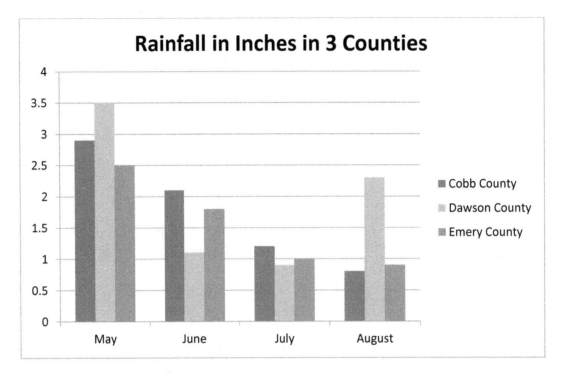

40) Approximately how many inches of rainfall did Cobb County have for July and August in total?
   A) 0.7 inches
   B) 0.9 inches
   C) 2 inches
   D) 3.2 inches

41) What was the approximate difference in the amount of rainfall for Dawson County and Emery County for June?
   A) Dawson County had 0.6 more inches of rainfall than Emery County.
   B) Emery County had 0.6 more inches of rainfall than Dawson County.
   C) Dawson County had 1.1 fewer inches of rainfall than Emery County.
   D) Emery County had 1.1 fewer inches of rainfall than Dawson County.

42) What was the approximate total rainfall for Emery County for all four months?
   A) 6.2 inches
   B) 6.8 inches
   C) 7.0 inches
   D) 7.4 inches

Look at the information below and answer questions 43 to 45.

A recipe of the ingredients needed to make 4 brownies is provided below.

> Brownie recipe
>
> ¼ cup of flour
> ½ cup of sugar
> ¼ cup of butter
> 3 tablespoons of cocoa powder
> ¼ teaspoon of baking powder
> ½ teaspoon of vanilla extract

43) How much sugar is needed to make 2 brownies?
    A) ¼ cup
    B) ¾ cup
    C) 1 cup
    D) 2 cups

44) How much vanilla extract is needed to make 6 brownies?
    A) ¼ teaspoon
    B) ¾ teaspoon
    C) 1¼ teaspoons
    D) 1½ teaspoons

45) How much cocoa powder and baking powder together is needed to make 12 brownies? (1 tablespoon = 3 teaspoons)
    A) 9¼ teaspoons
    B) 27¼ teaspoons
    C) 27½ teaspoons
    D) 27¾ teaspoons

WONDERLIC BASIC SKILLS VERBAL PRACTICE TEST 4

For questions 1 to 5, choose the answer that is the best synonym or antonym for the underlined word.

1) Earnest most nearly means the opposite of:
   A) masculine
   B) insincere
   C) athletic
   D) capable

2) Adept most nearly means:
   A) efficient
   B) skilled
   C) awkward
   D) inept

3) Indignant most nearly means:
   A) offended
   B) angry
   C) worried
   D) excited

4) Furor most nearly means:
   A) leader
   B) sorrow
   C) commander
   D) outcry

5) Jovial most nearly means:
   A) supportive
   B) sincere
   C) caring
   D) cheerful

For questions 6 to 9, choose the word that best indicates the meaning of the underlined word.

6) Her story was full of <u>hyperbole</u>.
   A) enchantment
   B) preoccupation
   C) exaggeration
   D) exhilaration

7) He might find it hard to make friends at college because he is so <u>studious</u>.
   A) bookish
   B) aloof
   C) selfish
   D) serious

8) The vacation that they had planned failed to <u>materialize</u>.
   A) be enjoyable
   B) prevail
   C) continue
   D) happen

9) They operate a <u>legitimate</u> business activity.
   A) prosperous
   B) defunct
   C) profitable
   D) lawful

For questions 10 to 14, choose the word that best completes the sentence.

10) His father's death _____ his decision to take over the family business.
   A) precipitated
   B) changed
   C) prevented
   D) overcame

11) The country's _____ policy is controlled by the Federal Reserve.
   A) monetary
   B) economy
   C) profitable
   D) remunerative

12) She was _____ with many duties and responsibilities.
   A) accompanied
   B) overjoyed
   C) fettered
   D) blessed

13) They were looking forward to the _____ of their new boss.
   A) season
   B) advent
   C) takeover
   D) birth

14) All applicants must undergo a _____ background investigation.
   A) stringent
   B) brief
   C) handy
   D) capable

For questions 15 to 18, read the text below and answer the questions that follow.

Bicycle Safety

Bicycling is an excellent way to exercise, see the natural world, and reduce your carbon footprint. However, bicyclists face many hazards, especially when they share the road with vehicles. Injuries can and do happen, even on a designated cycling path.

The number of deaths from bicycle incidents increased thirty percent from 2010 to the present. Of these bicyclist deaths, seventy percent involved motor vehicles. There are now approximately 80 million bicyclists on the road with motorized vehicles, so it is of paramount importance that bicyclists take safety precautions to protect themselves.

Cyclists would be imprudent not to check their equipment before setting out on any bike ride or journey. The seat should be adjusted and locked in place. It is best to have a rear-view mirror, a horn or bell, and reflectors on the rear, front, pedals, and spokes. When riding after dark, a bright headlight is also recommended.

The helmet is often worn incorrectly, thereby offering inadequate protection. It should be adjusted until it fits snugly on the head. Position the sizing pads so that the helmet fits properly. Then place the helmet level on your head, covering the forehead and not tipped backward or forward.

15) What situation does the author mention that is particularly dangerous for cyclists?
A) using designated cycling paths
B) failing to have a rear-view mirror
C) being on the road with automotive traffic
D) forgetting to wear a helmet

16) Why does the author mention deaths from cycling in paragraph 2?
A) to provide the reader with a shocking fact
B) to emphasize the importance of bicycle safety
C) to demonstrate how inconsiderate drivers of vehicles can be
D) to criticize those who do not ride and drive safely

17) Why does the author mention the adjustment of the helmet?
A) Too many people wear it covering the forehead.
B) Many people wear it incorrectly and ineffectively.
C) The helmet often fits too tightly and is uncomfortable.
D) People do not realize that the helmet can move backward or forward.

18) How does the author feel about checking cycling equipment?
A) It is tedious but necessary.
B) It should help to reduce cycling deaths in the future.
C) Drivers of vehicles should be aware of cycling equipment precautions.
D) Failing to do so is irresponsible.

For questions 19 to 22, choose the part of the sentence that contains an error. If the sentence is correct as written, then choose "no error."

19) Born in <u>Hamlet,</u> North Carolina, John Coltrane was <u>arguably</u> one of the <u>most famous of</u> all jazz musicians <u>having played</u> the saxophone. <u>No error</u>

20) When a government <u>establishes</u> a public sector borrowing requirement, <u>it</u> raises money through the issuance <u>of</u> stocks and bonds, which not only increases its available funds <u>and</u> also forms part of the national debt. <u>No error</u>

21) A rope and pulley system, an everyday apparatus <u>that easily</u> lifts heavy items, <u>having</u> long been <u>recognized by</u> physicists as a useful <u>application of</u> applied force. <u>No error</u>

22) Great Danes, large hunting dogs that <u>were bred</u> <u>originally</u> by Germans, were <u>once</u> the <u>principle</u> companion animal for the wealthy. <u>No error</u>

For questions 23 to 27, choose the words that best complete the sentence.

23) I know you are normally very careful, but you _____ to be extra cautious when you travel.
   A) did need
   B) do need
   C) have needed
   D) did

24) Although I will leave this job tomorrow, I feel so happy _____ with such wonderful people.
   A) to have work
   B) to have worked
   C) to have been worked
   D) worked

25) Even though the three of you have argued, _____ shouldn't have hard feelings against her.
   A) you and he
   B) you and him
   C) him and you
   D) yours and his

26) I requested that my friend _____ to the party.
   A) to be invited
   B) be inviting
   C) to have been invited
   D) be invited

27) That form was compulsory, so _____ it in.
   A) you should have filled
   B) should you have filled
   C) should have you filled
   D) you should filled

For questions 28 to 31, read the text below and answer the questions that follow.

Did you know that flowers and bees share a symbiotic relationship? Yes, that's right! Bees benefit from flowers, but flowers could not flourish without bees. Most people know that flowers provide bees with the food that the insects need in order to survive. Bees consume the pollen in the flower, as well as the nectar, the sweet liquid substance that flowers produce to attract the bees.

Most bees are social insects that live in colonies of between 10,000 and 60,000 inhabitants. After they collect nectar and pollen from flowers, they fly back to these colonies. They use the nectar to create honey, which then can feed the entire colony.

On the other hand, bees also bring benefits to flowering plants, helping the plants to pollinate and therefore reproduce. Plants cannot seek out mates to create offspring in the same way that animals do. Flowers need to have agents, like bees, birds, and even the wind, to move their genetic material from one plant to another.

Flowering plants have the male part of their genes in their pollen, and when bees fly from flower to flower, they carry and deposit this pollen in other plants in the same species. In this way, flowering plants are able to create seeds and reproduce.

Without bees, pollination and reproduction would be impossible for most of our plant species, so the work of bees is essential to the ecosystems they in which they live. This means that we can also enjoy various types of fruits, vegetables, and other plant products that would not be available otherwise.

28) What is the main idea of the passage?
   A) Bees and flowers depend on each another.
   B) Pollination and reproduction are necessary for flowers and bees.
   C) The genes of bees and flowers are very different.
   D) Agents like birds and bees depend on flowers.

29) According to the passage, how do bees benefit from flowers?
   A) They can pollinate more extensively.
   B) They create food from flower pollen and nectar.
   C) They can be more social and attract bees to their colonies.
   D) They become an important part of the ecosystem.

30) According to the passage, why do flowers and other plants need bees?
A) to help bee colonies expand
B) to seek out new mates
C) to correct a genetic flaw
D) to develop seeds and duplicate

31) Why are we able to enjoy various types of fruits, vegetables, and other plant products?
A) Flowering plants have the male part of their genes in their pollen.
B) Flowering plants are able to create seeds and reproduce.
C) Bees assist in the process of plant pollination and reproduction.
D) Bees are essential to their ecosystems.

For questions 32 to 35, read the information below and answer the questions that follow.

Nassir has a busy work schedule and an active social life. His normal work schedule every week is from Monday to Friday, 8 am to 5 pm. Although it is sometimes necessary, he prefers not to work after 5:00 pm as he likes to visit with friends or take part in his hobbies during the evening. A chart of Nassir's commitments for the month of February is shown below.

Sunday	Monday	Tuesday	Wednesday	Thursday	Friday	Saturday
1	2	3 6:00 pm Personal training at gym	4 7:00 pm Meet Ali in town	5 Staff meeting at work 1:30 pm	6 8:00 pm Martial arts practice	7
8	9 **Work from 1:00 pm to 9:00 pm this week**	10 8:30 am Personal training at gym	11 Staff meeting at work 3:30 pm	12 9:30 am Personal training at gym	13 10:00 am Meet Marta for brunch	14 8:00 am Go on hike with Martin and Suki
15 5:00 pm Meet Ali in town	16 8:00 pm Meet Terri for a late supper	17 7:00 pm Martial arts practice	18 8:30 pm Personal training at gym	19 7:30 pm Event at public library	20 6:00 pm Meet Jacinta for coffee	21 Go to Mom and Dad's this weekend
22 2:00 pm Meet Ali in town	23 **Work from 1:00 pm to 5:00 pm this week**	24 6:30 pm Meet Tom for supper	25 6:00 pm Meet Jacinta for coffee	26 Staff meeting at work 2:00 pm	27 8:00 am Martial arts practice	28 10:00 am Meet Jim for bike ride

32) Excluding his parents, how many people has Nassir named in his plans for this month?
A) 6
B) 7
C) 8
D) 9

33) Based on the information provided, which of the following statements best explains how Nassir plans the time that he spends exercising?
A) Nassir's gym is open 24 hours a day, so he can go there any time.
B) Nassir's martial arts practice typically takes place during the evening.
C) Nassir does not like to exercise early in the morning.
D) Nassir likes to exercise with friends when possible.

34) During the month of February, which of the following activities did Nassir take part in at least four times?
A) Meeting friends for supper.
B) Meeting friends for coffee or brunch.
C) Meeting Ali in town.
D) Personal training at the gym.

35) Which of the following statements is best supported by the information provided?
A) Nassir has staff meetings once a week.
B) Nassir normally sees his parents once a month.
C) Nassir finds it difficult to work late in the evening.
D) Nassir writes his work hours on his calendar only when they vary from 8 am to 5 pm.

For questions 36 to 41, read the text below and make any necessary corrections.

Dear Team:

(1) Thank you for your continuing hard work and dedication. **(2)** There are some exciting changes coming to our department that I wish to alert you to.

(3) Due to Maxim Inc.'s recent acquisition of our company, the executive management had decided that some restructuring of our department is in order so that our transition through this merger can be as seamless as possible.

(4) This is, in general, very good news for all of us since we will be taking ten new sales representatives on board. **(5)** This increase in staff would both relieve our current understaffing situation and prepare us for the heightened sales operations that this merger is anticipated to trigger.

(6) I am scheduling a staff meeting for tomorrow from 12 pm to 1 pm which I will outline the steps of this important transition; lunch will be provided.

(7) Please feel free to reach out to me at any time during the next few weeks with any question or concerns.

Best regards,

Darnell Hobbs
Email: dhobbs@maximinc.com

36) What change, if any, is needed in sentences 1 and 2?
   A) Change the second period to a question mark.
   B) Change "dedication" to "dedacation"
   C) Change "coming" to "are coming"
   D) Make no change

37) What change, if any, is needed in sentence 3?
   A) Change "had" to "has"
   B) Change "through" to "thru"
   C) Change "seamless" to "seemless"
   D) Make no change

38) What change, if any, is needed in sentence 4?
   A) Remove all commas.
   B) Change "since" to "yet"
   C) Change "is" to "was"
   D) Make no change

39) What change, if any, is needed in sentence 5?
   A) Change "would" to "will"
   B) Change "understaffing" to "understaffed"
   C) Change "that" to "which"
   D) Make no change

40) What change, if any, is needed in sentence 6?
   A) Change "which" to "when"
   B) Change "this" to "that"
   C) Change "anticipated" to "anticapated"
   D) Make no change

41) What change, if any, is needed in sentence 7?
   A) Change "reach out" to "reach"
   B) Change "any time" to "anytime"
   C) Change "question" to "questions"
   D) Make no change

For questions 42 to 44, choose the group of words that forms a complete sentence.

42) A) They're all here to report for duty.
   B) Pinching pennies and saving every day.
   C) Clearing up the issue once and for all.
   D) Even without considering all of the information.

43) A) Character flaws, warts and all.
   B) Being caring is in her nature.
   C) To honor her for her achievements.
   D) Living in New York while working as an actor.

44) A) Just as mother nature intended.
   B) Reading and swimming are favorite pastimes.
   C) Although you never intended to do so.
   D) Getting by in this world, in spite of its dangers.

For questions 45 to 47, choose the sentence in which the underlined word has the same meaning as it does in the original sentence.

45) The international <u>trade</u> agreement abolished taxes between the two nations.
A) The team will <u>trade</u> that baseball player for another.
B) Did you get a good <u>trade</u> in for your car?
C) The <u>trade</u> embargo will take effect next month.
D) His business did a good <u>trade</u> for many years.

46) If you <u>scratch</u> my back, I'll scratch yours.
A) There was a large <u>scratch</u> on the top of the dresser.
B) My speaking skills in Spanish really aren't up to <u>scratch</u>.
C) I always want to <u>scratch</u> mosquito bites, even though I shouldn't.
D) He had a <u>scratch</u> on his arm after doing all of the gardening.

47) The <u>produce</u> from that ranch is top-notch in quality.
A) I love eating berries and other fresh <u>produce</u> in the springtime.
B) I am going to need to work harder in order to <u>produce</u> the desired outcome.
C) She will help <u>produce</u> the movie by giving her time and money.
D) The factory will <u>produce</u> 100,000 units by the end of the year.

For questions 48 to 50, choose the new sentence that joins the original sentences in the best order.

48) Tom filled out the application form.
He sent it to the college.
He finally got his acceptance letter.
A) Once he filled out the application form, Tom finally got his acceptance letter after he had sent it in.
B) Sending his application form to college after filling it out, Tom finally got his acceptance letter.
C) Receiving his acceptance letter, Tom had filled out the application and sent it in.
D) After filling out the application form and sending it to college, Tom finally got his acceptance letter.

49) There was excessive rain yesterday.
Water began to gather in the streets.
The whole town was flooded.
A) Because the whole town was flooded, there was excessive rain yesterday and water began to gather in the streets.
B) There was excessive rain yesterday, so the whole town was flooded and water began to gather in the streets.
C) Due to excessive rain yesterday, which resulted in water beginning to gather in the streets, the whole town was flooded.
D) Water began to gather in the streets since the whole town was flooded with excessive rain yesterday.

50) The judge did not punish the criminal justly.
He decided to grant a lenient sentence.
This will not deter potential offenders in the future.
A) Instead of punishing the criminal justly and thereby sending out a message to deter potential offenders in the future, the judge decided to grant a lenient sentence.
B) Rather than granting a lenient sentence and punishing the criminal justly, the judge sent out a message to deter potential offenders in the future.
C) Although not granting a lenient sentence and punishing the criminal justly, the judge nevertheless did not send out a message to deter potential offenders in the future.
D) In order to grant a lenient sentence and punish the criminal justly, the judge sent out a message to deter potential offenders in the future.

ANSWERS AND EXPLANATIONS:

Quantitative Test 1

1) The correct answer is C. Remember that the order of operations is: Parentheses, Exponents, Multiplication, Division, Addition, and Subtraction, also known as PEMDAS. Our problems is: $82 + 9 \div 3 - 5 = ?$ In this problem, there are no operations with parentheses, exponents, or multiplication.
So, do the division first.
$9 \div 3 = 3$
Then replace this in the equation.
$82 + 9 \div 3 - 5 =$
$82 + 3 - 5 = 80$

2) The correct answer is A.
$52 + 6 \times 3 - 48 = ?$
This is another problem on the order of operations. There are no operations with parentheses or exponents, so do the multiplication first.
$6 \times 3 = 18$
Then put this number in the equation.
$52 + 6 \times 3 - 48 =$
$52 + 18 - 48 = 22$

3) The correct answer is C. We have to find the lowest common denominator (LCD) of the fractions. The LCD for this question is 15. We know this because the product of the other denominators is 3 times 5, which is 15. So, 15 is the lowest common denominator. We can illustrate the solution as follows:

Step 1 – Set up the original equation

$$\left(\frac{1}{3} + \frac{11}{5}\right) + \left(\frac{1}{15} - \frac{4}{5}\right) =$$

Step 2 – Convert denominators to the LCD

$$\left[\left(\frac{1}{3} \times \frac{5}{5}\right) + \left(\frac{11}{5} \times \frac{3}{3}\right)\right] + \left[\frac{1}{15} - \left(\frac{4}{5} \times \frac{3}{3}\right)\right] =$$

Step 3 – We can see clearly that the LCD is 15

$$\frac{5}{15} + \frac{33}{15} + \frac{1}{15} - \frac{12}{15}$$

4) The correct answer is C.
Convert the following to decimal format: $^3/_{20}$
In order to convert a fraction to a decimal, you must divide.

```
       .15
20)3.00
     2.0
     1.00
     1.00
        0
```

5) The correct answer is D. Our question was: 60 is 20 percent of what number? 20 percent is equal to 0.20. The phrase "of what number" indicates that we need to divide the two amounts given in the problem. $60 \div 0.20 = 300$. We can check this result as follows: $300 \times 0.20 = 60$

6) The correct answer is A. Our question was: $6^3/_4 - 2^1/_2 = ?$
If the fraction on the first mixed number is greater than the fraction on the second mixed number, you can subtract the whole numbers and the fractions separately. Remember to use the lowest common denominator on the fractions.
Subtract the whole numbers.
$6 - 2 = 4$
Subtract the fractions.
$^3/_4 - ^1/_2 =$
$^3/_4 - ^2/_4 =$
$^1/_4$
Now put them together for the result: $4^1/_4$

7) The correct answer is D.
Simplify the fractions:
$^{14}/_{18} = ^7/_9$
$^5/_{15} = ^1/_3$
$^2/_6 = ^1/_3$
Answer A is equal to $^7/_9$ and answers D and C are less than $^2/_3$.

8) The correct answer is D. Our problem is: $4^3/_8$ quarts $+ 3^7/_8$ quarts $= ?$
Step 1 – Add the whole numbers: $4 + 3 = 7$. Step 2 – Add the fractions: $3/8 + 7/8 = 10/8$. Step 3 – Simplify the fraction: $10/8 = 8/8 + 2/8 = 1 + 2/8 = 1^2/_8 = 1^1/_4$. Step 4 – Combine the results to solve: $7 + 1^1/_4 = 8^1/_4$

9) The correct answer is D. Convert the cups to quarter cups: 10 cups = 40 quarter cups. Then combine the whole number with the fraction and multiply to solve: $40^1/_4 \times 50$ cents per quarter cup $= 40.25 \times 0.50 = \$20.50$

10) The correct answer is A. Take the amount of money the customer gives you and subtract the amount of change provided to calculate the amount of the purchase: $160.00 – $12.64 = $147.36

11) The correct answer is C. The problem is asking for the total for all five months, so we add the amounts together to solve:
$723 + $618 + $576 + $812 + $984 = $3,713

12) The correct answer is A. Step 1 – Add the whole numbers: 37 + 25 = 62. Step 2 – Add the fractions: 2/5 + 4/5 = 6/5 = 1¹/₅. Step 3 – Combine these to get your new mixed number to solve the problem: 62 + 1¹/₅ = 63¹/₅

13) The correct answer is B. From the formula, we can see that 1 milligram = 0.001 gram. We are converting milligrams to grams, so multiply by 0.001 to solve: 1,275,000 milligrams × 0.001 = 1,275 grams

14) The correct answer is A. Our problem is: $^1/_8 \div {}^4/_3$ = ?
When you are asked to divide fractions, first you need to invert the second fraction. This means that you swap the numerator with the denominator. Then you multiply this inverted fraction by the first fraction given in the problem.
$^4/_3$ inverted is $^3/_4$
Then multiply the numerators and the denominators together to get the new fraction.

$$\frac{1}{8} \div \frac{4}{3} =$$

$$\frac{1}{8} \times \frac{3}{4} = \frac{3}{32}$$

15) The correct answer is B. Take the number of questions missed and add the extra credit points. –36 + 25 = –11. Since the question is asking how much the score was lowered, you need to give the amount as a positive number.

16) The correct answer is B. Convert the fractions in the mixed numbers to decimals: $^3/_4$ = 3 ÷ 4 = 0.75 and $^1/_5$ = 1 ÷ 5 = 0.20
Then represent the mixed numbers as decimal numbers.
Person 1: 14³/₄ = 14.75
Person 2: 20¹/₅ = 20.20
Person 3: 36.35
Then add all three amounts to solve: 14.75 + 20.20 + 36.35 = 71.30

17) The correct answer is C. To represent a fraction as a decimal, you need to divide. So, you will need to do long division to determine the answer.

```
     .10
50)5.00
    5.00
       0
```

18) The correct answer is D.   The sum of the work from all four people must be equal to 100%, simplified to 1. In other words, they make up the total hours by working together.
$A + B + C + D = 1$
$^1/_6 + ^1/_3 + ^1/_6 + D = 1$
Now find the lowest common denominator of the fractions.
The fractions for Person A and Person C already have 6 in their denominators, so we only have to convert the fraction for Person B.
$3 \times 2 = 6$, so the lowest common denominator is 6.
Convert the second fraction as required.
$^1/_3 \times ^2/_2 = ^2/_6$
Now add the fractions together.
$^1/_6 + ^2/_6 + ^1/_6 + D = 1$
$^4/_6 + D = 1$
$^4/_6 - ^4/_6 + D = 1 - ^4/_6$
$D = 1 - ^4/_6$
$D = ^2/_6$
$D = ^1/_3$

19) The correct answer is D. 20 percent is equal to 0.20. We are doing a reverse percentage, so we need to divide to solve: $60 ÷ 0.20 = $300. We can check this result as follows: 300 × 0.20 = 60

20) The correct answer is C. Divide and then round up: 82 people in total ÷ 15 people served per container = 5.467 containers. We need to round up to 6 since we cannot purchase a fractional part of a container.

21) The correct answer is D. The question is asking us about a time duration of 6 minutes, so we need to calculate the number of seconds in 6 minutes: 6 minutes × 60 seconds per minute = 360 seconds in total. Then divide the total time by the amount of time needed to make one journey: 360 seconds ÷ 45 seconds per journey = 8 journeys. Finally, multiply the number of journeys by the number of inches per journey in order to get the total inches: 10.5 inches for 1 journey × 8 journeys = 84 inches in total

22) The correct answer is A. Subtract whole numbers: 6 – 2 = 4. Then subtract fractions: $^3/_4 - ^1/_2 = ^3/_4 - ^2/_4 = ^1/_4$. Put them together for the result: $4^1/_4$

23) The correct answer is C. Step 1 – Take the 147 parts of blue slate chippings for this order and divide by the 3 parts stated in the original ratio: 147 ÷ 3 = 49. Step 2 – Multiply the result from Step 1 by the 2 parts of white gravel stated in the original ratio to get your answer: 49 × 2 = 98

24) The correct answer is A. The ratio of bags of apples to bags of oranges is 2 to 3, so for every two bags of apples, there are three bags of oranges. First, take the total amount of bags of apples and divide by the 2 from the original ratio: 44 ÷ 2 = 22. Then multiply this by 3 to determine how many bags of oranges are in the store: 22 × 3 = 66

25) The correct answer is D. For questions like this, you need to use the F-O-I-L method. This means that you multiply the terms two at a time from each of the two parts of the equation in this order:
First – Outside – Inside – Last
$(x + 3y)^2 = (x + 3y)(x + 3y)$

FIRST – Multiply the first term from the first set of parentheses with the first term from the second set of parentheses.
$(\boldsymbol{x} + 3y)(\boldsymbol{x} + 3y)$
$x \times x = x^2$

OUTSIDE – Multiply the first term from the first set of parentheses with the second term from the second set of parentheses.
$(\boldsymbol{x} + 3y)(x + \boldsymbol{3y})$
$x \times 3y = 3xy$

INSIDE – Multiply the second term from the first set of parentheses with the first term from the second set of parentheses.
$(x + \boldsymbol{3y})(\boldsymbol{x} + 3y)$
$3y \times x = 3xy$

LAST– Multiply the second term from the first set of parentheses with the second term from the second set of parentheses.
$(x + \boldsymbol{3y})(x + \boldsymbol{3y})$
$3y \times 3y = 9y^2$

Then we add all of the above products together to get the answer.
$x^2 + 3xy + 3xy + 9y^2 =$
$x^2 + 6xy + 9y^2$

26) The correct answer is A. If a term or variable is subtracted within the parentheses, you have to keep the negative sign with it when you multiply.
FIRST: $(x + 3y)(x - y)$
$x \times x = x^2$
OUTSIDE: $(x + 3y)(x - y)$
$x \times -y = -xy$
INSIDE: $(x + 3y)(x - y)$
$3y \times x = 3xy$
LAST: $(x + 3y)(x - y)$
$3y \times -y = -3y^2$
Then add all of the above once you have completed FOIL.
$x^2 - xy + 3xy - 3y^2 =$
$x^2 + 2xy - 3y^2$

27) The correct answer is B. Put in the values for x and y and multiply. Remember that two negatives together make a positive. For example,
$-(-5) = 5$
So, be careful when multiplying negative numbers.
$6x^2 - xy + y^2 =$
$(6 \times 5^2) - (5 \times -1) + (-1^2) =$
$(6 \times 5 \times 5) - (-5) + 1 =$
$(6 \times 25) + 5 + 1 =$
$150 + 5 + 1 = 156$

28) The correct answer is C.
Circumference = $\pi \times 2 \times$ radius.
In our question, the radius is 12, so the circumference is 24π.

29) The correct answer is D. Step 1 – Find the area of the ceiling. The area of a rectangle is (length × width). So, substitute the values to find the area: $(35 \times 25) = 875$ square feet. Step 2 – Find the area of each ceiling tile. The measurements for our tiles are given in inches: 6 inches by 6 inches = 36 square inches. Step 3 – Calculate how many square inches there are in a square foot: 12 inches by 12 inches = 144 square inches. Step 4 – Determine how many tiles you need per square foot: 144 square inches ÷ 36 square inches per tile = 4 tiles per square foot. Step 5 – Multiply to solve: 875 square feet in total × 4 tiles per square foot = 3,500 tiles needed

30) The correct answer is B. The area of circle M is $8^2\pi = 64\pi$. The area of circle M is 39π greater than the area of circle N, so subtract to find the area of circle N: $64\pi - 39\pi = 25\pi$. The area of circle N is calculated as follows: $5^2\pi = 25\pi$. So the radius of circle N is 5.

31) The correct answer is B. The formula for perimeter is as follows: P = 2W + 2L. The field is 12 yards by 10 yards, so we need 12 yards × 2 for the long sides field and 10 yards × 2 for the shorter sides: (2 × 10) + (2 × 12) = 20 + 24 = 44

32) The correct answer is B. Cone volume = (π × radius^2 × height) ÷ 3
volume = ($\pi 3^2$ × 4) ÷ 3 = ($\pi 9$ × 4) ÷ 3 = $\pi 36$ ÷ 3 = 12π

33) The correct answer is B. Bookcase A is 8 feet long and 2 feet deep, so multiply to solve: 8 × 2 = 16 square feet

34) The correct answer B. is Bookcase B is 5 feet long and two feet deep:
5 × 2 = 10 square feet

35) The correct answer is B. 70 square feet × $5.50 per piece = $385 total cost

36) The correct answer is C. Subtract the percentage of the discount from 100% to get the percentage of the price to be paid: 100% − 27.5% = 72.5%. Multiply to solve: $385 × 72.5% = $279.13

37) The correct answer is D. The total number of patients is 793,000 and 89% of them have survived, so multiply to solve: 793,000 × 0.89 = 705,770

38) The correct answer is. C. You need to determine the death rate, so subtract the survival rate from 100% to get the death rate for each category. Then multiply for each category and compare:
Cardiopulmonary and vascular deaths: 602,000 × 0.18 = 108,360
HIV/AIDS deaths: 215,000 × 0.27 = 58,050
Diabetes deaths: 793,000 × 0.11 = 87,230
Cancer and leukemia deaths: 231,000 × 0.52 =120,120
Deaths from premature birth complications: 68,000 × 0.36 = 24,480
So, cancer and leukemia caused the greatest number of deaths.

39) The correct answer is A. Refer to your calculations for the previous question and add the two smallest amounts together: 24,480 + 58,050 = 82,530

40) The correct answer is B. The line with the squares is the highest line for July. From the legend, we can see that this represents Company B.

41) The correct answer is A. The line with the squares for company B is at $1,400,000 for May. The line with the triangles for Company C is at

$600,000 for May. So, Company B's sales were $800,000 more than Company C's for May.

42) The correct answer is A. We can see that December has the highest figure for all three of the lines. Accordingly, December will also have the greatest combined sales for all three companies.

43) The correct answer is D. Reptiles account for 42% of the zoo creatures, and there are 1,500 creatures in total, so multiply to solve:
1,500 × 0.42 = 630 reptiles

44) The correct answer is B. At the start of the year, 26% of the zoo creatures were quadrupeds and 15% of the creatures were fish. So, solve by multiplying and subtracting as follows: (1500 × 0.26) − (1500 × 0.15) = 390 − 225 = 165 more quadrupeds than fish

45) The correct answer is C. We have to calculate the percentage of birds at the start of the year by subtracting the percentages for the other categories: 100% − 40% − 21% − 16% = 23%. The percentage of birds was 17% at the start of the year and 23% at the end of the year, so there was a 6% increase in the bird population. We can then multiply to solve: 1,500 × 0.06 = 90 more birds at the end of the year

Verbal Test 1

1) The correct answer is A. This is a form of the third conditional because it is talking about how a past event could have been changed, so the inverted form of the past perfect "had you studied" is the correct answer.

2) The correct answer is C. We are speaking about a repetitive, habitual action that is performed on the food, so the present simple passive tense (are not served) is needed in this sentence.

3) The correct answer is A. When we begin a sentence with a verb in the "ing" form like this, it is called a present participle phrase. Present participle phrases are used to introduce the main clause of the sentence, which mentions the topic of skiing.

4) The correct answer is C. We need the "would have been" + past participle sentence construction here because we are speaking retrospectively about how a past action could have had a different outcome.

5) The correct answer is C. The sentence construction in this question is similar to that of the previous question. We need "should have done" because we are speaking retrospectively about how he could have avoided eviction.

6) The correct answer is B. AMS-4994 is in the eighth row of the chart. Going across this row, we can see that the request date in the second column is 03/29.

7) The correct answer is B. Don't waste your time looking at all of the entries since we are only being asked about numbers 4995 to 4998. Number 4995 took 5 days to action, 4996 took 4 days, 4997 took 3 days, and 4998 took 5 days. Of course, you need to remember that there are 31 days in March when you are counting the days.

8) The correct answer is C. Be sure to look at the far-right column for the archive date. Number 4992 "Meet with Customer" was requested on April 6 and archived on June 8, so there were 24 days left in April, 31 days in May, and 8 days in June, for a total of 63 days.

9) The correct answer is D. The initial request was on March 26, and the final request was on April 9. So, there were 5 days in March and 9 days in April, for a total of 14 days.

10) The correct answer is D. *Acquiesce* means to comply to someone's wishes or to accommodate their requests.

11) The correct answer is C. *Patent* means obvious or apparent. It is most similar in meaning to the word *visible*.

12) The correct answer is A. Lenient means that you are forgiving or forbearing of another person's behavior, so it is closest in meaning to *easy-going*.

13) The correct answer is A. *Propitiate* means placate or pacify, so it is closest in meaning to the word *appease*.

14) The correct answer is C. *Pernicious* means malicious or damaging.

15) The correct answer is A. The phrase *engulfed in* is the best grammatically and colloquially, since it is the phrase that is most often used to describe fires.

16) The correct answer is B. *Contemplate* means to mull over or think about something deeply.

17) The correct answer is D. To be galvanized into action means that something makes you determined and resolute about achieving a goal.

18) The correct answer is: no error. The sentence contains no errors in grammar or usage.

19) The correct answer is: spanned. You need to add *is* before the word *spanned* in order to construct the verb correctly.

20) The correct answer is: used. The verb form should be *use*, which is the present simple tense. We need to use the present simple tense when we are describing a scientific principle, as in this sentence.

21) The correct answer is: it is. The grammatical subject of this clause of the sentence is *sparks*, which is plural. So, we should use *they are*, not *it is*.

22) The correct answer is D. Damaged packages should be placed into container E, regardless of their weight. This package has been erroneously placed into container B. The final paragraph states that if an item is placed into the wrong sorting container, there will be a delay of 5 days.

23) The correct answer is B. Container D is for all packages that are 80 ounces or more in weight.

24) The correct answer is C. The first paragraph states: In the middle of the room, we have placed a special staging station for international orders.

25) The correct answer is D. The sentence is correct as written.

26) The correct answer is A. When the word *however* is used in the middle of a sentence, it needs to be offset by commas.

27) The correct answer is C. The action in this sentence is the result of the action mentioned in the previous sentence. So, the word *therefore* is best.

28) The correct answer is C. The comma is not needed after the name of a country.

29) The correct answer is D. This is correct because the words "to export, to invest, and to grow financially" are all in the same grammatical form. They all have the word *to* in front of the verb.

30) The correct answer is B. The phrase "containing confidential information" describes the letter, so it needs to be placed directly after the word *letter.*

31) The correct answer is A. All of the key words in the phrase "increasing air pollution, decreasing fossil fuels, and controlling costs associated with rising inflation" are correctly in the -ing form.

32) The correct answer is D. A full sentence must have, at a minimum, a grammatical subject and a verb that describes the grammatical subject. Here we have the sentence: The restaurant closes at midnight. The grammatical subject is *the restaurant* and the verb is *closes.*

33) The correct answer is D. The sentence is: Off we go on another adventure! The grammatical subject is *we* and the verb is *go.* The sentence begins with the adverb *off* to heighten the exclamatory form.

34) The correct answer is C. The sentence is: He hopes to start this summer. The grammatical subject is *he* and the verb is *hopes.*

35) The correct answer is C. In the original sentence, the word *ache* is a verb that means to hurt. Sentence C is the only answer choice that also uses the word *ache* as a verb.

36) The correct answer is B. In the original sentence, the verb *comb* is used as a verb in its metaphorical sense, meaning to search meticulously. In the other answer choices, the word is used as a noun or as a verb in the literal sense.

37) The correct answer is C. In the original sentence, the word *fly* is used as a verb that refers to the literal action of being airborne. The word is used idiomatically or as a noun in the other sentences.

38) The correct answer is B. To get the maximum SPM for $3\frac{1}{2}$-ounce rayon fabric, we need to go to the second column of the first chart. The SPM of 720 is provided in the second row of the chart.

39) The correct answer is B. For 4-ounce (oz) light denim, we go to the fourth column and second row of the first table. Here, we can see that an SPM of 910 is recommended for this material. Then, you need to go to the footnote. Needle number 3 can be used for speeds up to 1200 SPM, so it is the correct answer.

40) The correct answer is D. 4-ounce tapestry cloth is in the third column and second row of the second tale. The SPM for this fabric is 1940, so looking at the footnote, we see that we need needle #4, since it goes up to speeds of 2000 SPM.

41) The correct answer is C. Floral design is good for the mind because people have to visualize and think about how to organize the flowers. The text explains that floral design requires "its participants to focus on visual skills." Notice that the question is asking about floral design in particular, rather than flowers in general.

42) The correct answer is D. Flower arranging is good for seniors because it helps them be more socially active with other people. The text says that flowers "have the most positive impact upon seniors, reducing depression and encouraging interaction with others."

43) The correct answer is B. The author feels that flowers can have a positive effect on almost anyone. The text concludes as follows: "studies like these seem to confirm what I have always known instinctively: that having flowers makes us feel better in many ways."

44) The correct answer is A. This sentence makes the most sense and also has the correct cause-and-effect relationship.

45) The correct answer is A. The sentence begins with the idea of the length of the training, so it provides the best contrast. It is also the best grammatically.

46) The correct answer is B. The sentence begins with the idea of the acrimonious relationships, so it provides the best contrast. It is also the best grammatically.

47) The correct answer is A. The word *temperamental* refers to someone who is irritable or easily upset.

48) The correct answer is B. A precedent creates a criterion or paradigm. So, it is closest to the word *exemplar*.

49) The correct answer is A. *Commend* means to credit someone with an achievement or to acclaim or praise an achievement.

50) The correct answer is C. The word *ostensibly* has the same meaning as the words *evidently* or *supposedly*.

Quantitative Test 2

1) The correct answer is A. Subtract the whole numbers and the fractions separately. Do the whole numbers first: 5 – 2 = 3. In The find the lowest common denominator for the fraction: 1/2 – 1/4 = (1 × 2)/(2 × 2) – 1/4 = 2/4 – 1/4 = 1/4 . Therefore, the result is 3¼.

2) The correct answer is B. Be sure to put the decimal point in the correct position after you do the multiplication. If we remove the decimal points:
655 × 12 = (655 × 10) + (655 × 2) = 6550 + 1330 = 7860
6.55 has a decimal two places from the right. 1.2 has a decimal point 1 place from the right. So, adding these together, we have to put the decimal point three numbers from the right on the final product of 7860. Therefore, the final answer is 7.860, which is simplified to 7.86

3) The correct answer is A. Step 1 – First, you need to find the result in decimal format: 404 ÷ 6 = 67.33. Step 2 – Take the whole number before the decimal point in your result and multiply it by the divisor, which is the number after the "divide by" sign: 67 × 6 = 402. Step 3 – Subtract the result from step 2 from the dividend. The dividend is the number before the "divide by" sign: 404 – 402 = 2

4) The correct answer is A. 12 × 8 = 96, so we know our answer must be something close to 8. Divide to get the solution: 99 ÷ 12 = 8.25

5) The correct answer is B. Add the numbers, being sure to carry the one's in the hundreds and thousands places when you add up by hand.

   1,832
   + 791
   2,623

6) The correct answer is B. Divide and convert to a percentage as shown:
1/16 = 1 ÷ 16 = 0.0625; 0.0625 = 6.25%

7) The correct answer is C. Add the four figures together to solve: 163.75 + 107.50 + 91.25 + 10.30 = 372.80

8) The correct answer is D. For practical estimation problems like this, round the numbers up or down to the nearest thousand. 13,975 is rounded up to 14,000 and 1,135 is rounded down to 1,000. Then add to get the total distance from top to bottom: 14,000 + 1,000 = 15,000

9) The correct answer is C. Step 1 – Take the total number of employees and divide this by 5: 250 ÷ 5 = 50. Step 2 – The question asks how many questionnaires have not been completed and returned, so subtract to find the amount in the 'not returned' subset: 5 – 4 = 1. Step 3 – Multiply the result from step 2 by the result from step 1 to solve: 50 × 1 = 50

10) The correct answer is D. Step 1 – Determine the total for sales in December: $20 × 55 = $1,100. Step 2 – Determine the total sales for January: $12 × 20 = $240. Step 3 – Add these two amounts to solve: $1,100 + $240 = $1,340

11) The correct answer is A. Step 1 – First of all, we need to deduct the difference from the total: 540 – 52 = 488. So, there were 488 passengers on both flights combined, plus the 52 additional passengers on the morning flight. Step 2 – Now divide this result by 2 to allocate the number of passengers to each flight. 488 ÷ 2 = 244 passengers on the evening flight

12) The correct answer is D. The plumber is going to earn $4,000 for the month. He charges a set fee of $100 per job, and he will do 5 jobs, so we can calculate the total set fees first: $100 set fee per job × 5 jobs = $500 total set fees. Then deduct the set fees from the total for the month in order to determine the total for the hourly pay: $4,000 – $500 = $3,500. He earns $25 per hour, so divide the hourly rate into the total hourly pay in order to determine the number of hours he will work: $3,500 total hourly pay ÷ $25 per hour = 140 hours to work

13) The correct answer is D. Step 1 – Add the whole numbers: 19 + 14 = 33. Step 2 – Add the fractions: 3/4 + 3/4 = 6/4. Step 3 – Simplify the fraction from Step 2 – 6/4 = $1^2/_4$ = $1^1/_2$. Step 4 – Combine the results from Step 1 and Step 3 to solve the problem: 33 + $1^1/_2$ = $34^1/_2$

14) The correct answer is D. We know that Mary has already gotten 80% of the money. However, the question is asking how much money she still needs. 100% – 80% = 20% and 20% = .20 Now do the multiplication: 650 × .20 = 130

15) The correct answer is D. Express the fractions in the lowest common denominator and subtract to solve: $^1/_3$ – $^1/_7$ = $^7/_{21}$ – $^3/_{21}$ = $^4/_{21}$

16) The correct answer is C. Calculate the discount: $15 – $12 = $3. Divide this into the original price to get the percentage: $3 ÷ $15 = 0.20 = 20%

17) The correct answer is D. Set up each part of the problem as an equation. The museum had twice as many visitors on Tuesday (T) as on Monday (M), so T = 2M. The number of visitors on Wednesday exceeded that of Tuesday by 20%, so W = 1.20 × T. Then express T in terms of M for Wednesday's visitors: W = 1.20 × T = 1.20 × 2M = 2.40M. Finally, add the amounts together for all three days: M + 2M + 2.40M = 5.4M

18) The correct answer is D. Step 1 – Find the area of the ceiling. The area of a rectangle is (length × width). So, substitute the values to find the area: (35 × 25) = 875 square feet. Step 2 – Find the area of each ceiling tile. The measurements given in inches: 6 inches by 6 inches = 36 square inches. Step 3 – Calculate how many square inches there are in a square foot: 12 inches by 12 inches = 144 square inches. Step 4 – Determine how many tiles you need per square foot: 144 square inches ÷ 36 square inches per tile = 4 tiles per square foot. Step 5 – Multiply to solve: 875 square feet in total × 4 tiles per square foot = 3,500 tiles needed

19) The correct answer is B. From the formula sheet, we can see that 1 milligram = 0.001 gram. We are converting milligrams to grams, so we are doing the formula in the correct order, rather than in reverse. Therefore, multiply by 0.001 to solve: 1,275,000 milligrams × 0.001 = 1,275 grams

20) The correct answer is B. At the beginning of January, there are 300 students, but 5% of the students leave during the month, so we have 95% left at the end of the month: 300 × 95% = 285. Then 15 students join on the last day of the month, so we add that back in to get the total at the end of January: 285 + 15 = 300. If this pattern continues, there will always be 300 students in the academy at the end of any month.

21) The correct answer is D. Calculate the discount: $120 × 12.5% = $15 discount. Then subtract the discount from the original price to determine the sales price: $120 – $15 = $105

22) The correct answer is A. The ratio of Item Y to Item X is 1 to 20. So, the units in Item Y form one group and the units of Item X form another group. Therefore, the total units can be divided into groups of 21. Accordingly, $1/21$ of the units are of Item Y. The factory produced 11,235 units last week, so we calculate as follows: 11,235 × $1/21$ = 535

23) The correct answer is A. In order to answer questions on ordering numbers from least to greatest or greatest to least, remember that when two fractions have the same numerator, the fraction with the smaller number in the denominator is the larger fraction. So, $-1/4$ is less than $1/8$, $1/8$ is less than $1/6$, and $1/6$ is less than 1.

115

24) The correct answer is B. They buy 4 of product A at $5 each, so they buy $20 worth of product A. They paid $60 in total, so subtract the total cost of product A from the overall total to calculate the total spent on Product B: $60 − $20 = $40. Product B costs $8 each, so divide to solve: $40 spent on Product B ÷ $8 each = 5 units

25) The correct answer is D. Step 1 – Determine the percentage of the discount on Product A: $4 discount ÷ $20 original price = 20% discount. Step 2 – Calculate the dollar value of the discount on Product B: $16 × 20% = $3.20. Step 3 – Subtract the dollar value of the discount on Product B from the normal price to get the discounted price of Product B: $16 − $3.20 = $12.80

26) The correct answer is C. Since there are 60 seconds in a minute, and pulse is measured in 10 second units, we divide the seconds as follows: 60 ÷ 10 = 6. Accordingly, the PPM is calculated by talking P times 6: PPM = P6

27) The correct answer is D. The PPM is calculated as in the previous problem. In order to find the excess amount, we deduct the ideal PPM of 60 from the patient's actual PPM: PPM − 60

28) The correct answer is C. She bought 3 pairs of shoes, so determine the amount spent on shoes: 3 pairs of shoes × $25 each= $75. Then deduct this from the total amount of the purchase to calculate how much she spent on socks: $85 − $75 = $10. The socks cost $2 a pair, so divide to solve: $10 ÷ $2 each = 5 pairs

29) The correct answer is C. Step 1 – Determine the price per yard: $10.50 per 1/2 yard × 2 = $21.00 per yard. Step 2 – Calculate the price for 20 yards: 20 × $21.00 = $420.00. Step 3 – The customer purchased 20 and a half yards, so the price of the remaining half yard is $10.50. Add this to the result from Step 2 to get your answer: $420.00 + $10.50 = $430.50

30) The correct answer is D. To solve this type of problem, do the multiplication on the items in parentheses first.
$5x − 2(x + 3) = 0$
$5x − 2x − 6 = 0$

Then deal with the integers by putting them on one side of the equation as follows:
$5x − 2x − 6 + 6 = 0 + 6$
$3x = 6$

Then solve for x.

$3x = 6$

$x = 6 \div 3$

$x = 2$

31) The correct answer is B. The total amount available is $55,000, so we can substitute this for C in the equation provided in order to calculate R number of residents:

$C = \$750R + \$2,550$

$\$55,000 = \$750R + \$2,550$

$\$55,000 - \$2,550 = \$750R + \$2,550 - \$2,550$

$\$55,000 - \$2,550 = \$750R$

$\$52,450 = \$750R$

$\$52,450 \div \$750 = \$750R \div \$750$

$\$52,450 \div \$750 = R$

$69.9 = R$

It is not possible to accommodate a fractional part of one person, so we need to round down to 69 residents.

32) The correct answer is D. Subtract the lengths of the shorter sides from the total: $350 - 75 - 75 = 200$. Divide this by two to get the length of each of the other sides: $200 \div 2 = 100$

33) The correct answer is B. The measurement of a straight line is 180° so the measurement of angle A is 180° − 109° = 71°. Since this is an isosceles triangle, angle A and angle B are equal. The sum of the degrees of the three angles of any triangle is 180°, so we subtract to find the measurement of angle A: 180° − 71° − 71° = 38°.

34) The correct answer is B. The health and other categories were the lowest, so add them together to solve: 11% + 9% = 20%

35) The correct answer is D. Take the total dollar amount and multiply by the 27% for education: $5,275,300 × 0.27 = $1,424,331

36) The correct answer is C. Take the total dollar amount of the budget and multiply by the 21% for public safety: $6,537,200 × 0.21 = $1,372,812

37) The correct answer is D. Calculate the length of strapping for the piece that goes around the front of the package: 22 + 42 + 22 + 42 = 128. Then calculate the length of strapping for the piece that goes over the top of the package: 20 + 42 + 20 + 42 = 124. Then add the 15 inches for the handle: 128 + 124 + 15 = 267 total inches

38) The correct answer is C. Without the handle, we need 128 + 124 = 252 inches per package. 252 inches per package × 25 packages = 6,300 total inches

39) The correct answer is C. To calculate cubic inches, we take the height times the depth times the length: 20 × 22 × 42 = 18,480 cubic inches

40) The correct answer is D. At 11:00, thirty minutes (or half an hour) will have passed. If he is traveling 70 miles per hour, he will have traveled 35 miles in this half hour (70 × ½ = 35). If he was 140 miles from Farnam when he saw the sign, we need to subtract 35 miles from this to get the answer: 140 − 35 = 105 miles from Farnam

41) The correct answer is C. At 12:30, two hours will have passed and he will have traveled 140 miles (70 miles per hour × 2 hours = 140 total miles). Georgetown was 210 miles away when he saw the sign, so subtract to find out how far he is from Georgetown: 210 − 140 = 70 miles from Georgetown

42) The correct answer is C. From the previous question, we know that at 12:30 he is 70 miles from Georgetown without having taken a break. If he is traveling 70 miles per hour, he would need only 1 more hour to get to Georgetown at 1:30 if he had not taken a break. But we need to add in a 30 minute break, so he would arrive in Georgetown at 2:00 pm.

43) The correct answer is D. We can see that SUV's account for the lowest number of accidents on each of the two dates. So, SUV's will also account for the lowest combined total for the two dates.

44) The correct answer is A. The chart shows that cars account for the largest number of accidents on each of the four dates represented. So, cars will also account for the largest combined total for all four dates.

45) The correct answer is D. On May 1, pick-ups were involved in 7 accidents, and on June 1, they were involved in 10 accidents. So, for the two dates combined, pick-ups had 17 accidents.

Verbal Test 2

1)   The correct answer is C. The construction "not to spend" correctly states the professor's request as an admonishment.

2)   The correct answer is D. The other answer options do not provide the correct form of the word *opening* as a verb. So, we need to choose answer D, which uses the word *opening* correctly as a noun.

3)   The correct answer is C. The verb *should* correctly expresses the obligation that Janet was under.

4)   The correct answer is D. Answers A and C are incorrect since the preposition *from* is not needed. Answer B does not have the correct word order.

5)   The correct answer is C. The word *advocate,* when used as a noun, refers to someone who promotes or supports a certain issue. *Judge* is too formal in this instance, and *arbiter* refers to someone who arbitrates or acts as a go-between.

6)   The correct answer is B. *Laud* means to praise or honor someone for his or her actions.

7)   The correct answer is C. The word *dubious* refers to something that is unreliable or questionable in quality.

8)   The correct answer is A. *Perturb* means to disturb or annoy someone.

9)   The correct answer is A. *Alacrity* means enthusiasm or readiness, especially when approaching a task that needs to be done.

10)   The correct answer is D. *Dormant* refers to something that is inactive or abeyant.

11)   The correct answer is D. Ingenious refers to an idea that is original and clever.

12)   The correct answer is B. *Toxic* means poisonous or harmful to the health.

13)   The correct answer is C. The other answers do not make sense grammatically or lexically.

14)   The correct answer is A. Extenuating circumstances are those that lessen, mitigate, or excuse the seriousness of a situation.

15) The correct answer is C. The word *nebulous* refers to something that is unclear.

16) The correct answer is C. Data processing is in the third row of the second day. Class 2 registrations are in the far right column, with 776 people.

17) The correct answer is B. The registrations are in the second and fourth columns. Scanning the data, we can see that the largest number is 1,378 for "Other Peripherals" on Day 1.

18) The correct answer is B. The maximum number of participants is shown in columns 1 and 3. Word Processing on Day 2 is the smallest at 815 maximum participants.

19) The correct answer is B. Remember that a complete sentence needs a grammatical subject and a verb. *Getting home* is a gerund that is used as the subject of the sentence, and the main verb is the word *is*.

20) The correct answer is A. This sentence is written in the imperative voice since it is giving a command. The main verb is *try* and the grammatical subject is implied from the context as the word *you*.

21) The correct answer is C. The grammatical subject is *car* and the main verb is *would be*.

22) The correct answer is: effected. We need the verb here that means "to impact upon," so we should use the word *affected* instead.

23) The correct answer is: constitute. We are speaking about a singular action, so we need the singular verb form *constitutes*.

24) The correct answer is: that. We should use the plural pronoun *those* instead, since the grammatical subject is the word *settlers*, which is also plural.

25) The correct answer is B. There is no ostensible order for the way that the letters are used on the map.

26) The correct answer is A. There are probably too many interior walls and doors for the premises to be used as a restaurant.

27) The correct answer is B. The premises are currently used as offices, and area F is the common area that leads to all of the other interior spaces, so it would be suitable for a receptionist.

28) The correct answer is D. "Frustrated, fed up, and tired" uses all of the verbs as past participles.

29) The correct answer is B. This sentence correctly uses the comma after the modifying phrase. Sentence A lacks the comma. Sentence C is not correct grammatically, and sentence D is in the passive voice, so it does not have the correct emphasis.

30) The correct answer is C. This is the only sentence that correctly uses the grammatical subject *you* in both clauses of the sentence.

31) The correct answer is D. The main idea of the passage is that the athletic performance of some animals is superior to that of humans. The text states: "the athletic training and performance of human beings seem unimpressive, paling in comparison to the phenomenal feats performed naturally by members of the animal kingdom."

32) The correct answer is A. People sometimes need special diving equipment because the human body is not designed to cope underwater like fish can. The text states: "However, the human body can withstand underwater depths up to only 2,300 feet." "Withstand" means able to cope.

33) The correct answer is B. The author feels that the athletic performance of animals is remarkable and extraordinary. The author uses words like "phenomenal" to describe animal performance, but uses the words "unimpressive" and "paltry" to describe the performance of humans.

34) The correct answer is D. The third sentence states that "swimwear . . . cannot be returned in any circumstance as per state health and hygiene laws."

35) The correct answer is A. The last sentence states: "Since we now perform damage checks on merchandise at the point of sale, as of today, we will no longer offer refunds for any item that is damaged."

36) The correct answer is A. A bikini is swimwear, so it cannot be returned. The damage is not an excuse because of the new damage policy, stated in the last sentence.

37) The correct answer is C. We need to form a defining clause with the word *which*.

38) The correct answer is A. *For instance* is used as an introductory phrase, so we should place a comma after it.

39) The correct answer is D. We are contrasting the idea of a young population in this sentence to the idea of an elderly population in the previous sentence.

40) The correct answer is C. The possessive form is not needed since the word *families* is used as a noun.

41) The correct answer is D. Remember that the singular form is needed if you use the word *or* in a grammatical subject, as in the phrase "disease epidemic or natural disaster."

42) The correct answer is B. *Staying alert* is a gerund phrase which is used as the grammatical subject of this sentence.

43) The correct answer is A. The sentence is in the imperative voice since it gives a command. The pronoun *you* (for the person receiving the command) is understood from the context.

44) The correct answer is C. The grammatical subject is *vacationing* and the main verb is *can come.*

45) The correct answer is B. In both sentences, the word *iron* is used as a noun to refer to the metallic substance. Sentence A refers to a home appliance, while sentences C and D use *iron* as a verb.

46) The correct answer is B. The verb *milk* is used metaphorically to mean taking advantage of a situation. In sentences A and D, we are talking about the dairy drink, and in sentence C, *milk* is used literally as a verb.

47) The correct answer is B. The word *matter* is used in both sentences as a noun that refers to the topic under consideration. In sentence A, we use the word *matter* in its scientific sense. In sentence C, the word is used in a metaphorical sense, and in sentence D the word is used as a verb.

48) The correct answer is A. This is the only option that gives the clauses of the sentence in the correct order that states the cause-and-effect relationship.

49) The correct answer is C. This sentence places the correct emphasis on his dislike of alcohol and is also correct grammatically.

50) The correct answer is D. This is the only option that gives the clauses of the sentence in the correct order that states the cause-and-effect relationship.

Quantitative Test 3

1) The correct answer is B. 12 ÷ 80 = 0.15
   Be sure to put the decimal point in the correct place in your answer.

2) The correct answer is D. Perform the division, and then check the decimal places of the numbers. Divide as follows: 1523.48 ÷ 100 = 15.2348. Reading our result from left to right: 1 is in the tens place, 5 is in the ones place, 2 is in the tenths place, 3 is in the hundredths place, 4 is in the thousandths place, and 8 is in the ten-thousandths place.

3) The correct answer is A. Line all of the decimal points up for problems like this. Put in zeros where necessary, as follows:

   0.280
   0.028
   0.208
   0.820

   When you have them lined up like this, you can see that 0.028 is the smallest one.

4) The correct answer is A. Be careful with decimal point position when you do multiplication problems on the test: 6.83 × 5.2 = 35.516. We can see that 6.83 has two decimal places, and 5.2 has one decimal place, so there are three decimal places in our answer.

5) The correct answer is C. Subtract the whole numbers: 4 – 3 = 1
   The lowest common denominator for the fractions is 10.
   $^1/_2 - {}^2/_5 =$
   $[^1/_2 \times {}^5/_5] - [^2/_5 \times {}^2/_2] =$
   $^5/_{10} - {}^4/_{10} =$
   $^1/_{10}$

   The put the whole number and fraction back together for your answer:
   $1^1/_{10}$

6) The correct answer is B. Add the numbers, being sure to carry the one's in the hundreds and thousands places when you add up by hand.

   1,832
   + 791
   ‾‾‾‾‾
   2,623

7) The correct answer is B. Divide and convert to a percentage as shown:
1/16 = 1 ÷ 16 = 0.0625
0.0625 = 6.25%

8) The correct answer is B. Divide the total amount by the sales price per unit to solve: $7,375 ÷ $59 = 125 units sold

9) The correct answer is C. Divide and then express the result as a percentage. Step 1 – Treat the line in the fraction as the division symbol: 6/25 = 6 ÷ 25 = 0.24. Step 2 – To express the result from Step 1 as a percentage, move the decimal point two places to the right and add the percent sign: 0.24 = 24%

10) The correct answer is D. Calculate the total, and divide by the number of days. Step 1 – Find the total: $90 + $85 + $85 + $105 + $110 = $475. Step 2 – Divide the result from Step 1 by the number of days: $475 ÷ 5 = $95

11) The correct answer is D. Step 1 – Add up the fractions: 3/4 + 1/2 = 3/4 + 2/4 = 5/4. Step 2 – Simplify the fraction – 5/4 = 4/4 + 1/4 = $1^1/_4$ = 1 foot and 3 inches. Step 3 – Combine the results from Step 1 and Step 3 to solve the problem: 15 feet + 1 foot and 3 inches = 16 feet and 3 inches

12) The correct answer is C. Step 1 – Convert $28^3/_{10}$ for subtraction: $28^3/_{10}$ = $27^3/_{10}$ + 1 = $27^3/_{10}$ + $^{10}/_{10}$ = $27^{13}/_{10}$. Step 2 – Subtract the whole numbers. You have spent $7^9/_{10}$ hours on the job so far, so subtract the 7 hours: 27 – 7 = 20. Step 3 – Subtract the fractions: 13/10 – 9/10 = 4/10. Step 4 – Simplify the fraction from Step 3 – 4/10 = (4 ÷ 2)/(10 ÷ 2) = 2/5. Step 5 – Combine the results from Step 2 and Step 4 to get your new mixed number to solve the problem: 20 + 2/5 = $20^2/_5$

13) The correct answer is C. Step 1 – Determine the total amount of inches of material needed for one unit. Don't forget that the second material needs to be doubled because there is a double layer of this material: 18 + 19 + 19 = 56 inches. Step 2 – Calculate how many inches are needed in total: 56 inches per unit × 18 units = 1008 inches in total. Step 3 – Convert the inches to feet: 1008 inches ÷ 12 = 84 feet

14) The correct answer is D. Step 1 – Add the whole numbers: 49 + 18 = 67. Step 2 – Add the fractions: 3/16 + 1/16 = 4/16 = 1/4. Step 3 – Combine the results to get your new mixed number to solve the problem: 67 + 1/4 = $67^1/_4$

15) The correct answer is D. Step 1 – Take the total amount of flour required for this batch and divide by the 9 stated in the original ratio: $126 \div 9 = 14$. Step 2 – Take the amount from Step 1 and multiply by 2 from the original ratio to solve the problem: $14 \times 2 = 28$

16) The correct answer is B. Step 1 – Calculate the amount of time spent on the initial job: 12:10 to 2:25 = 2 hours and 15 minutes = 135 minutes. Step 2 – Calculate the rate per cap: 135 minutes $\div$ 3 caps = 45 minutes per cap. Step 3 – Calculate how many minutes there are in 9 hours: 9 hours $\times$ 60 minutes = 540 minutes. Step 4 – Divide to solve: 540 minutes available $\div$ 45 minutes per cap = 12 caps

17) The correct answer is D. Add the percentages together to solve: $58\% + 27\% = 85\%$

18) The correct answer is B. Take the amount of defective chips and divide by the amount of total chips: $11 \div 132 = 0.083 = 8.3\%$, which we round to 8%.

19) The correct answer is D. Step 1 – Determine the excess amount over the amount for the deal: 100 bottles needed – (4 cases $\times$ 24 bottles each) = 100 – 96 = 4 individual bottles left. Step 2 – Take the result from the previous step and multiply by the individual price: $4 \times \$2.50 = \$10$. Step 3 – Determine the cost of the 4 cases: $4 \times \$50 = \$200$. Step 4 – Add the results from the previous two steps to get the total wholesale price for the deal: $\$200 + \$10 = \$210$

20) The correct answer is B. Isolate the x variable in order to solve the problem.
$5x - 4(x + 2) = -2$
$5x - 4x - 8 = -2$
$x - 8 = -2$
$x - 8 + 8 = -2 + 8$
$x = 6$

21) The correct answer is B. Substitute 5 for the value of x to solve.
$x^2 + xy - y = 41$
$5^2 + 5y - y = 41$
$25 + 5y - y = 41$
$25 - 25 + 5y - y = 41 - 25$
$5y - y = 16$
$4y = 16$
$4y \div 4 = 16 \div 4$
$y = 4$

22) The correct answer is B. Since A counts for 35% of the final grade, we set 35% to a decimal and put the decimal in front of the variable so that the variable will have the correct weight. So, the value of test A is 0.35A. Test B counts for 65%, so the value of test B is 0.65B. The final grade is the sum of the values for the two tests. So, we add the above products together to get our equation: 0.35A + 0.65B

23) The correct answer is A. Miles per hour (MPH) is: miles ÷ hours = MPH So, if we have the MPH and the miles traveled, we need to change the above equation in order to calculate the hours.
miles ÷ hours = MPH
miles ÷ hours × hours = MPH × hours
miles = MPH × hours
miles ÷ MPH = (MPH × hours) ÷ MPH
miles ÷ MPH = hours
In other words, we divide the number of miles by the miles per hour to get the time for each part of the race. So, for the first part of the race, the hours are calculated as follows: 80 ÷ 5
For the second part of the race, we take the remaining mileage and divide by the unknown variable: $20 ÷ x$
Since the race is divided into two parts, these two results added together equal the total time.
Total time = $[(80 ÷ 5) + (20 ÷ x)]$
The total amount of miles for the race is then divided by the total time to get the average miles per hour for the entire race.
That is because MPH is calculated as follows:
MPH = miles ÷ hours
We have a 100 mile race, so the result is:
$100 ÷ [(80 ÷ 5) + (20 ÷ x)]$

24) The correct answer is A. Put in the values for x and y and multiply.
$2x^2 + 3xy - y^2 =$
$(2 × 3^2) + (3 × 3 × - 3) - (-3^2) =$
$(2 × 3 × 3) + (3 × 3 × - 3) - (-3 × -3) =$
$(2 × 9) + (3 × -9) - (9) =$
$18 + (-27) - 9 =$
$18 - 27 - 9 =$
$18 - 36 =$
-18

25) The correct answer is D. The two people are working at different costs per hour, so each person needs to be assigned a variable. A is for the number of hours for the first person, and B is for the number of hours for the second person. The cost for each person is calculated by taking the number of hours that the person works by the hourly wage for that person. So, the equation for wages for the first person is $(7.25 \times A)$
The equation for the wages for the second person is $(10.50 \times B)$
The total cost of the wages for this job is the sum of the wages of these two people. $(7.25 \times A) + (10.50 \times B) = (7.25A + 10.50B)$

26) The correct answer is C. The formula for perimeter is $2(L + 2)$.
$2(18 + 10) = 56$

27) The correct answer is D. The perimeter of a rectangle is $2(length + width)$. So, determine the total width for both sides: $2 \times 75 = 150$. Now deduct this amount from the perimeter: $350 - 150 = 200$. Finally, divide this result by 2 to get the length: $200 \div 2 = 100$

28) The correct answer is D. Circumference $\approx$ diameter $\times 3.14$. The circumference of the first circle is calculated as follows: diameter $\times 3.14 = 10 \times 3.14 = 31.4$. The circumference of the second circle is as follows: diameter $\times 3.14 = 6 \times 3.14 = 18.84$. The difference in the circumferences is: $31.4 - 18.84 = 12.56$

29) The correct answer is D. The volume of a box is calculated by taking the length times the width times the height: $5 \times 6 \times 10 = 300$

30) The correct answer is B. Cone volume $= (3.14 \times radius^2 \times height) \div 3$. Substitute the values for base and height. volume $= (3.14 \times 3^2 \times 4) \div 3 = (3.14 \times 9 \times 4) \div 3 = 3.14 \times 36 \div 3 = 37.68$

31) The correct answer is B. Remember that the perimeter is the measurement along the outside edges of the rectangle or other area. The formula for perimeter is as follows: $P = 2W + 2L$. If the room is 12 feet by 10 feet, we need 12 feet $\times$ 2 to finish the long sides of the room and 10 feet $\times$ 2 to finish the shorter sides of the room. $(2 \times 10) + (2 \times 12) = 20 + 24 = 44$. Each piece of wood is one foot long, so 44 pieces are needed to finish the room.

32) The correct answer is B. We can see from the chart that there are 4 bars that are 1 mile each. This distance occurs more frequently than any other.

33) The correct answer is A. The best distance was 1.5 miles and the worst distance was 0.8 mile. So, subtract to solve: $1.5 - 0.8 = 0.7$

34) The correct answer is A. You can do the computation quickly from the introduction, which states: An athlete ran 10 miles in 1.5 hours. 1.5 hours is equal to 90 minutes, and there are 10 miles, so on average, it took 9 minutes to do each mile. (90 ÷ 10 = 9)

35) The correct answer is A. Count the sides of the squares on the gray part of the diagram: Left = 5; Bottom = 3 + 1 = 4, Right = 2 + 3 = 5; Top = 4. Then add up: 5 + 4 + 5 + 4 = 18. Alternatively, visually go around the gray figure and count up the outside edges of the gray squares.

36) The correct answer is C. First, calculate the total area represented on the diagram: 9 × 7 = 63 square yards in total. Then count the gray squares for the reservoir. We can see that there are 18 gray squares. Then subtract to solve: 63 – 18 = 45 square yards

37) The correct answer is A. We know from the calculations in the previous question that the gray area is 18 square yards and the white area is 45 square yards. So, the ratio is 18:45. Both of these numbers are divisible by 9, so we can simplify the ratio to 2:5 (18 ÷ 9 = 2 and 45 ÷ 9 = 5).

38) The correct answer is A. The temperature was 13 degrees on Friday, which was higher than any other temperature.

39) The correct answer is C. The temperature was –10° on Sunday, which was the lowest that week.

40) The correct answer is C. 13 – –10 = 23. Be sure to subtract the low from the high, rather than the high from the low.

41) The correct answer is B. To calculate an average, you need to add up all of the values. Then divide this sum by the number of items. So, we need to add up all of the temperatures and divide by 7:
–10 + –9 + 1 + 6 + 8 + 13 + 12 = 21; 21 ÷ 7 = 3

42) The correct answer is C. Add up the amounts in the far right column:
12 + 20 + 32 + 32 = 96

43) The correct answer is D. Part 3 had 35 total questions and part 4 had 45 total questions, so add to solve: 35 + 45 = 80

44) The correct answer is A. Chantelle correctly answered 12 out of 15 questions, so she incorrectly answered 3 questions (15 – 12 = 3). This can be expressed as the fraction 3/15, which can be simplified to 1/5.

45) The correct answer is B. First calculate how many correct answers there were: 12 + 20 + 32 + 32 = 96. Then calculate how many questions were on the test in total: 15 + 25 + 35 + 45 = 120. Finally, divide to solve 96 ÷ 120 = 0.80 = 80%

Verbal Test 3

1) The correct answer is C. We need to use the word *suitable* as an adjective to describe the level of the lecture.

2) The correct answer is C. We use the phrase "taller than" to compare him to his three siblings.

3) The correct answer is A. The main verb *completed* is in the past simple tense, so we need to use *brought*, which is also in the past simple tense.

4) The correct answer is D. We need to use the past perfect form *had accepted* because we are describing two actions in the sentence, and the acceptance preceded his feeling.

5) The correct answer is D. *Servility* means enslavement, servitude, or subjugation.

6) The correct answer is C. *Indispensable* means essential, crucial, or fundamental. It is the opposite of *superfluous*.

7) The correct answer is B. A sycophant is someone who uses flattery or servility to win another person's favor.

8) The correct answer is C. *Upheaval* means disturbance, disruption, or disorder.

9) The correct answer is B. *Exonerate* means to be pardoned or acquitted of a charge.

10) The correct answer is A. Since most people don't wear this kind of clothing, it would be considered unconventional.

11) The correct answer is C. *Acrimony* means discord or animosity.

12) The correct answer is A. *Intricate* in this context means detailed or complex.

13) The correct answer is D. The mouse and keyboard are peripherals since they are connected to the CPU.

14) The correct answer is B. This part of the book deals with computer hardware, so is should discuss the care and maintenance of the hardware.

15) The correct answer is A. The acknowledgements section is where the author acknowledges or thanks the people who helped with the publication of the book.

16) The correct answer is B. Radium is used as a cancer treatment because it destroys cancerous cells. The last sentence explains that radium "eradicates malignant cells without any lasting ill effects on the body." "Eradicate" and "destroy" are synonyms. You may be tempted to choose answer C, but it is incorrect because radium can have positive long-term effects for cancer patients.

17) The correct answer is D. For main idea questions, as well as for questions on selecting a title for a selection, you will need to choose an answer that is neither too general nor too specific. Answers A and C are much too general since the passage does not focus on the entire life and work of Madame Curie. Answer B is too specific because cancer treatment is mentioned in only the last paragraph. Therefore, "The Discovery and Use of Radium" is the best title for the passage.

18) The correct answer is B. For "opinion vs. fact" questions like this, look for modal verbs (should, would, may, might) and superlative adjectives that express opinions (the best, the most, etc). The notion whether someone should be an inspiration to others is a matter of personal opinion, so B is the best answer.

19) The correct answer is: from. The verb *differentiate* should be used with the preposition *to*, not *from*.

20) The correct answer is: had been. We are talking about a completed action in the past that is of historical significance, so the past simple tense *was* should be used, rather than the past perfect *had been*.

21) The correct answer is: seems. The grammatical subject of the sentence is *comets*, which is plural, so we need the verb *seem*, rather than *seems*.

22) The correct answer is: their. The word *chicory* is singular, so we need to use *its* instead of *their*.

23) The correct answer is C. The introductory phrase is correctly placed and uses both present participles (drafting and serving) in the correct -ing form.

24) The correct answer is D. This is the only sentence that has the correct cause-and-effect relationship.

25) The correct answer is C. This sentence uses the past participle phrase "overworked and underpaid" correctly and also places the comma after the phrase.

26) The correct answer is C. The fourth point of the first list states: "Write your signature and the date on the 10% Guest Discount for Meals Ticket."

27) The correct answer is B. The first point of the second list states: "The member must accompany his or her guest for a spa treatment."

28) The correct answer is D. The first sentence gives the following explanation: "Any club member who holds an Elite Status Card will now get discounts off the price of guest admissions, in addition to the other rewards and perks of the Elite Status program."

29) The correct answer is B. The grammatical subject of this exclamation is *we* and the main verb is *go*. The adverb *away* is placed at the head of the sentence to give the proper emphasis to the exclamation.

30) The correct answer is A. The sentence has a compound grammatical subject: The old, the new, the borrowed, and the blue. The main verb is the word *are*.

31) The correct answer is C. The gerund *talking* is the grammatical subject and the main verb is *can lead*.

32) The correct answer is C. A question is posed since we begin the construction with the following words: *Did you know*

33) The correct answer is A. The phrase *of course* needs to be offset by a comma since it is an interjection in the sentence.

34) The correct answer is C. The grammatical subject of the sentence is *organically-grown food*, so we need the phrase *it is* to use the correct singular form.

35) The correct answer is B. The words *the use of* are repetitive since we have already used the word *using* earlier in the construction.

36) The correct answer is A. Without the change, we have a comma splice. In other words, we are incorrectly joining two independent clauses as the sentence is written.

37) The correct answer is B. The change is needed to have the correct spelling of the word *virulent*.

38) The correct answer is B. In both sentences, the word *trust* is used as a verb to mean placing faith in someone. Sentences A and C use the word as a noun, while sentence D uses the word as an adjective.

39) The correct answer is C. In both sentences, the word *present* is used as an adjective to describe the attendance of someone at an event. Sentence A uses the word as a noun, sentence B uses the word as a verb, and sentence D uses the word to describe time, not attendance.

40) The correct answer is D The word *report* is correctly used in both of these sentences as a verb. Sentences A and B use the word as a noun referring to a written or spoken text, while sentence C uses the word as a noun in a different sense to refer to a noise.

41) The correct answer is B. This sentence uses the word *certain* to show that prerequisites do apply to some classes. This idea is erroneously omitted in Sentence A. Sentence C and D are verbose and poorly constructed.

42) The correct answer is A. This sentence is the only one with the correct cause-and-effect construction.

43) The correct answer is A. Sentences B and D suggest an erroneous cause-and-effect relationship, while sentence C is too terse.

44) The correct answer is B. The author mentions that high cholesterol can be caused by drinking coffee. The text says that "we have known for a few years now that coffee can elevate blood pressure and also lead to high cholesterol."

45) The correct answer is C. Coffee can cause stomach ache because it makes acidity levels in the stomach higher. The text explains that "coffee stimulates the secretion of gastric acid, which can lead to stomach upset."

46) The correct answer is A. The author mentions anxiety and depression to exemplify another problem caused by drinking too much coffee. We know this because it describes "health problems like anxiety and depression."

47) The correct answer is C. *Clemency* means mercy or compassion.

48) The correct answer is A. *Abridge* means to shorten or condense a piece of writing.

49) The correct answer is A. *Stalwart* means dependable and fearless.

50) The correct answer is B. *Entice* means to attract or beguile someone.

Quantitative Test 4

1) The correct answer is D. Change the double negative to a positive number to solve: $- (-5) + 3 = 5 + 3 = 8$

2) The correct answer is C. The question asks us to estimate $502 \div 49.1$. We round 502 down to 500 and we round 49.1 up to 50. So, our answer is 10 since $500 \div 50 = 10$

3) The correct answer is C. The question is: $^1/_3 \times ^2/_3 = ?$. Multiply the numerator by the numerator and the denominator by the denominator: $^1/_3 \times ^2/_3 = {}^{1 \times 2}/_{3 \times 3} = ^2/_9$

4) The correct answer is D. Both the numerator and denominator are divisible by 3, so simplify to solve: $12/27 = (12 \times 3) / (27 \times 3) = 4/9$

5) The correct answer is D. First, subtract the integers on the mixed numbers: $3 - 2 = 1$. Then convert the fractions: 1/2 is equal to 3/6 and 1/3 is equal to 2/6. So, we can subtract as shown: $3/6 - 2/6 = 1/6$. Combine these results for your answer: $1 + 1/6 = 1^1/_6$

6) The correct answer is B. If they lost 20 percent of the games, then they won 80 percent of them. So, multiply to solve: $50 \times 80\% = 50 \times 0.80 = 40$

7) The correct answer is A. Multiply 90 by 4 to get the total number of points and undo the erroneous operation: $90 \times 4 = 360$. Then divide by 5 to get the correct average: $360 \div 5 = 72$

8) The correct answer is C. Divide the 800 total students by the 20 students in the ratio: $800 \div 20 = 40$. Then multiply this by the 17 in the ratio to solve: $40 \times 17 = 680$

9) The correct answer is B. Divide the number of straight-A students into the total number of students in the class: $2 \div 25 = 0.08 = 8\%$

10) The correct answer is D. Step 1 – Take the total amount of Item G required for this batch and divide by the 7 stated in the original ratio: $147 \div 7 = 21$. Step 2 – Take the amount from Step 1 and multiply by 2 from the original ratio to solve the problem: $21 \times 2 = 42$

11) The correct answer is B. Step 1 – Calculate the amount of time spent on the initial job: 1:10 to 3:25 = 2 hours and 15 minutes = 135 minutes. Step 2 – Calculate the rate per item: 135 minutes ÷ 3 items = 45 minutes

per item. Step 3 – Calculate how many minutes there are in 9 hours: 9 hours × 60 minutes = 540 minutes. Step 4 – Divide to solve: 540 minutes available ÷ 45 minutes per item = 12 items

12) The correct answer is D. Add the percentages together to solve: 29% + 17% = 46%

13) The correct answer is C. The twelve students who failed the test represent one-third of the class. Since one-third of the students have failed, we can think of the class as being divided into three groups. Group 1: The 12 students who failed; Group 2: 12 students who would have passed; Group 3: 12 more students who would have passed. So, the class consists of 36 students in total. In other words, we need to multiply by three to find the total number of students: 12 × 3 = 36

14) The correct answer is C. Yesterday the train traveled $117\frac{3}{4}$ miles, and today it traveled $102\frac{1}{6}$ miles. Because the fraction on the first mixed number is greater than the fraction on the second mixed number, we can subtract the whole numbers and the fractions separately.
Step 1 – Subtract the whole numbers: 117 – 102 = 15 miles.
Step 2 – Perform the operation on the fractions by finding the lowest common denominator: $\frac{3}{4}$ miles – $\frac{1}{6}$ miles = ? In order to find the LCD, we would normally need to find the common factors first. In this problem, the LCD is 12 since 3 × 4 = 12 and 2 × 6 = 12. So, we express the fractions in their LCD form: $\frac{3}{4} \times \frac{3}{3} = \frac{9}{12}$ and $\frac{1}{6} \times \frac{2}{2} = \frac{2}{12}$. Then subtract these two fractions: $\frac{9}{12} - \frac{2}{12} = \frac{7}{12}$. Step 3 – Combine the results from the two previous steps to solve the problem: $117\frac{3}{4}$ miles – $102\frac{1}{6}$ miles = $15\frac{7}{12}$ miles.

15) The correct answer is D. We round 1.07 up to 1.1, then round 2.46 up to 2.5 and 3.92 down to 3.9. Then add to solve: 1.1 + 2.5 + 3.9 = 7.5

16) The correct answer is D. A percentage can always be expressed as a number with two decimal places. For example, 15% = 0.15 and 20% = 0.20. In our problem, 16% = 0.16. So D is correct.

17) The correct answer is B. Step 1 – First of all, you need to calculate the amount of the discount: $18 original price × 40% = $18 × 0.40 = $7.20 discount. Step 2 – Then deduct the amount of the discount from the original price to calculate the sales price of the item: $18 original price – $7.20 discount = $10.80 sales price.

18) The correct answer is C. Step 1 – Calculate the amount of remaining stock in quarts and ounces: [2 × (16 cups and 7 ounces)] + [3 × (20 cups and 4 ounces)] = 32 cups and 14 ounces + 60 cups and 12 ounces = 92 cups and 26 ounces. Step 2 – Convert the existing stock from cups to quarts: 1 quart = 4 cups, so divide the amount of cups by 4 to convert to quarts: (92 cups ÷ 4) + 26 ounces = 23 quarts and 26 ounces. There are 32 ounces in a quart, so we cannot convert the remaining 26 ounces to quarts. Step 3 – Calculate the amount required to restock. 50 quarts are required in total, and you have approximately 23 quarts on hand, so subtract to find out how many more quarts you need to get the stock back up to 50 quarts: 50 – 23 = 27 quarts needed. Step 4 – The chemical comes in 5-quart containers, so calculate how many containers you need to buy to cover the 27 quarts that are required: 27 ÷ 5 = 5.4 quarts. It is not possible to buy a fractional part of a container, so you have to buy 6 containers.

19) The correct answer is D. Step 1 – Calculate the volume of each vat: length × width × height = 10 × 10 × 12 = 1,200 cubic feet. Step 2 – Determine how full each vat is in terms of cubic feet. Vat 1: 1,200 × $^3/_4$ = 1,200 × 0.75 = 900 cubic feet. Vat 2: 1,200 × $^4/_5$ = 1,200 × 0.80 = 960 cubic feet. Step 3 – Add the volume of the two vats together to determine the total volume: 900 + 960 = 1,860 cubic feet. Step 4 – Convert the cubic feet to cubic inches. 1 cubic foot = 1,728 cubic inches, so we multiply to convert: 1,860 cubic feet × 1,728 = 3,214,080 cubic inches. Step 5 – Multiply by the price to solve: 3,214,080 cubic inches × $0.12 = $385,689.60, which we round to $385,690.

20) The correct answer is C. Step 1 – Determine the total number of hours: 7.5 hours per day for 2 days = 7.5 × 2 = 15 hours. Step 2 – Calculate the profit your company makes per hour. The customer was billed $75 per hour for your work, and you were paid $40 per hour: $75 – $40 = $35 profit per hour. Step 3 – Multiply the total number of hours by the profit per hour to solve: 15 hours × $35 profit per hour = $525

21) The correct answer is D. Step 1 – Add the whole numbers: 4 + 3 = 7. Step 2 – Add the fractions: 3/8 + 7/8 = 10/8. Step 3 – Simplify the fraction from Step 2 – 10/8 = 8/8 + 2/8 = 1 + 2/8 = $1^2/_8$ = $1^1/_4$. Step 4 – Combine the results from Step 1 and Step 3 to solve the problem: 7 + $1^1/_4$ = $8^1/_4$

22) The correct answer is C. In this problem, the fraction on the second number is larger than the fraction on the first number, so we need to convert the first fraction before we start our calculation. Step 1 – Convert $12^7/_{16}$ for subtraction: $12^7/_{16}$ = $11^7/_{16}$ + 1 = $11^7/_{16}$ + $^{16}/_{16}$ = $11^{23}/_{16}$.

Step 2 – There were 8⁹/₁₆ yards left, so subtract the whole numbers: 11 – 8 = 3. Step 3 – Subtract the fractions: 23/16 – 9/16 = 14/16. Step 4 – Simplify the fraction from Step 3 – 14/16 = (14 ÷ 2)/(16 ÷ 2) = 7/8. Step 5 – Combine the results from Step 2 and Step 4 to get your new mixed number to solve the problem: 3 + 7/8 = 3⁷/₈

23) The correct answer is B. The problem tells us the relative number of units sold, but the question is asking for the relative number of units left. So, subtract the decimal from 1 to find the relative number left: 1 – 0.75 = 0.25. Then multiply the total number of items at the start by this decimal number: 80 items × 0.25 = 80 × 0.25 = 20 items left

24) The correct answer is D. First of all, you need to determine the difference in temperature during the entire time period: 62 – 38 = 24 degrees less. Then calculate how much time has passed. From 5:00 PM to 11:00 PM, 6 hours have passed. Next, divide the temperature difference by the amount of time that has passed to get the temperature change per hour: 24 degrees ÷ 6 hours = 4 degrees less per hour. To calculate the temperature at the stated time, you need to calculate the time difference. From 5:00 PM to 9:00 PM, 4 hours have passed. So, the temperature difference during the stated time is 4 hours × 4 degrees per hour = 16 degrees less. Finally, deduct this from the beginning temperature to get your final answer: 62°F – 16°F = 46°F

25) The correct answer is C. We can see from the formula sheet that we have a formula to convert meters to centimeters and another formula to convert inches to centimeters, so we will need to use those two formulas to solve the problem. Step 1 – Determine the measurement in centimeters: 1 meter = 100 centimeters. Step 2 – Convert the centimeters to inches. The formulas states that 1 inch = 2.54 centimeters. However, we need to use the formula in reverse because we are converting centimeters to inches. So, divide to solve: 100 ÷ 2.54 = 39.37 inches

26) The correct answer is A. Add up the candy in each of the three bags: 43 + 28 + 31 = 102. Then divide by the 34 students: 102 ÷ 34 = 3

27) The correct answer is A. Divide the total cost by the price per square foot: $281,250 ÷ 250 = 1125. Ignore the information about the down payment as it is only intended to distract you.

28) The correct answer is B. In our problem, if $t\%$ subscribe to digital TV packages, then $100\% - t\%$ do not subscribe. In other words, since a percentage is any given number out of 100%, the percentage of students who do not subscribe is represented by this equation: $(100\% - t\%)$. This equation is then multiplied by the total number of students (n) in order to determine the number of students who do not subscribe to digital TV packages: $(100\% - t\%) \times n$

29) The correct answer is B. Substitute 12 for the value of x. Then simplify and solve.
$x^2 + xy - y = 254$
$12^2 + 12y - y = 254$
$144 + 12y - y = 254$
$144 - 144 + 12y - y = 254 - 144$
$12y - y = 110$
$11y = 110$
$11y \div 11 = 110 \div 11$
$y = 10$

30) The correct answer is A.
FIRST: $(\mathbf{3x} + y)(\mathbf{x} - 5y) = 3x \times x = 3x^2$
OUTSIDE: $(\mathbf{3x} + y)(x - \mathbf{5y}) = 3x \times -5y = -15xy$
INSIDE: $(3x + \mathbf{y})(\mathbf{x} - 5y) = y \times x = xy$
LAST: $(3x + \mathbf{y})(x - \mathbf{5y}) = y \times -5y = -5y^2$
Then add all of the above once you have completed FOIL:
$3x^2 - 15xy + xy - 5y^2 = 3x^2 - 14xy - 5y^2$

31) The correct answer is A. The factors of 9 are: $1 \times 9 = 9$; $\mathbf{3} \times 3 = 9$. The factors of 3 are: $1 \times \mathbf{3} = 3$.
So, put the integer for the common factor outside the parentheses first:
$9x^3 - 3x = 3(3x^3 - x)$
Then determine if there are any common variables for the terms that remain in the parentheses.
For $(3x^2 - x)$ the terms $3x^2$ and x have the variable x in common. So, now factor out x to solve: $3(3x^3 - x) = 3x(3x^2 - 1)$

32) The correct answer is D. The original price of the sofa on Wednesday was x. On Thursday, the sofa was reduced by 10%, so the price on Thursday was 90% of x or $0.90x$. On Friday, the sofa was reduced by a further 15%, so the price on Friday was 85% of the price on Thursday, so we can multiply Thursday's price by 0.85 to get our answer: $(0.90)(0.85)x$

33) The correct answer is C. The sum of all three angles inside a triangle is always 180 degrees. So, we need to deduct the degrees given from 180° to find out the total degrees of the two other angles: 180° − 36° = 144°. Now divide this result by two in order to determine the degrees for each angle: 144° ÷ 2 = 72°

34) The correct answer is B. No lights are to be installed in the corners, so each of the two 10-feet walls will have 1 light installed in the middle of each wall: 10 ÷ 5 = 2, but we subtract 1 from this for the corner. So, we have 1 light on each of the 2 shorter walls, which accounts for 2 lights so far. Each of the 25-foot walls have 5 increments of 5 feet, and again no lights are in the corners: (25 ÷ 5) − 1 = 4. So, each of the 2 long walls will have 4 lights on each wall. So there will be 10 lights in total on the walls in the room. (1 + 1 + 4 + 4 = 10). You may wish to draw a diagram on your scratch paper when solving problems like this one.

35) The correct answer is B. You are being asked about the distance around the outside, so you need to calculate the perimeter, Write out the formula: (length × 2) + (width × 2). Then substitute the values: (5 × 2) + (3 × 2) = 10 + 6 = 16

36) The correct answer is B. The area of circle A is 0.4^2 × 3.14 = 0.16 × 3.14 = 0.5024. The area of circle B is 0.2^2 × 3.14 = 0.04 × 3.14 = 0.1256. Then subtract: 0.5024 − 0.1256 = 0.3768

37) The correct answer is B. We know from the formula that triangle area = base × height ÷ 2. The triangle has a base of 4 and a height of 15. Substitute values to solve: 4 × 15 ÷ 2 = 30

38) The correct answer is C. An equilateral triangle has three equal sides and three equal angles. Since all 3 angles in any triangle need to add up to 180 degrees, each angle of an equilateral triangle is 60 degrees (180 ÷ 3 = 60). Angles that lie along the same side of a straight line must add up to 180. So, we calculate angle *a* as follows: 180 − 60 = 120

39) The correct answer is D. The formula for the area of a circle is: πR^2.
The area of circle A is $\pi \times 5^2 = 25\pi$ and the area of circle B is $\pi \times 3^2 = 9\pi$. So, the difference between the areas is 16π.
The formula for circumference is: $\pi 2R$. The circumference of circle A is $\pi \times 2 \times 5 = 10\pi$ and the circumference for circle B is $\pi \times 2 \times 3 = 6\pi$. The difference in the circumferences is 4π. So, answer D is correct.

40) The correct answer is C. Cobb County is the darkest bar, so it is the first bar for each month. For July, Cobb County had 1.2 inches of rain, and in August it had 0.8 inches, so it had 2 inches in total for the two months.

41) The correct answer is B. In June, Dawson County had 1.1 inches of rain and Emery County had 1.7 inches. Therefore, Emery County had 0.6 more inches of rainfall than Dawson County.

42) The correct answer is A. Emery County had the following amounts of rainfall: May = 2.5 inches; June = 1.8 inches; July = 1 inch; August = 0.9 inch. Then add these amounts together to solve: 2.5 + 1.8 + 1 + 0.9 = 6.2 inches in total

43) The correct answer is A. The recipe is for 4 brownies, but we only want to make 2 brownies, so we have to use half of the ingredients. ½ cup of sugar is needed for the original recipe, but we only want half of this: ½ × ½ = ¼

44) The correct answer is B. The original recipe was for 4 brownies but we are making 6 brownies, so we can set up the following fraction to get our proportion: 6/4 = 4/4 + 2/4 = 1 + ½ = 1½. So for 6 brownies, we need to use 1½ of all of the ingredients listed on the original recipe: ½ teaspoon × 1½ = [(½ × 1) + (½ × ½)] = ½ + ¼ = ¾

45) The correct answer is D. 3 tablespoons of cocoa powder and ¼ teaspoon of baking powder are needed for the original recipe to make 4 brownies. There are 3 teaspoons in a tablespoon, so calculate the total teaspoons needed for the original recipe first: 3 tablespoons × 3 = 9 teaspoons cocoa powder + ¼ teaspoon baking powder = 9¼ teaspoons in total. We are now making 12 brownies, so we need to multiply all of the ingredients by 3: 9¼ × 3 = 27¾ teaspoons

Verbal Test 4

1) The correct answer is B. *Earnest* means sincere or heartfelt.

2) The correct answer is B. *Adept* means extremely capable or proficient.

3) The correct answer is A. If someone is indignant about something, he or she is annoyed and resentful.

4) The correct answer is D. A furor over something means that there is a commotion or outburst.

5) The correct answer is D. *Jovial* means having a cheerful or jolly disposition.

6) The correct answer is C. *Hyperbole* means exaggeration or overstatement.

7) The correct answer is A. The word *studious* refers to someone who is inclined to study, so it is closest in meaning to *bookish*.

8) The correct answer is D. In this context, *materialize* means to take place or come to fruition.

9) The correct answer is D. *Legitimate* means appropriate, authorized, or lawful.

10) The correct answer is A. *Precipitate* means to bring about or cause something, especially to do so quickly.

11) The correct answer is A. *Monetary policy* refers to a country's regulations surrounding finance.

12) The correct answer is C. The phrase *fettered with* means burdened with or constrained by.

13) The correct answer is B. The word *advent* is synonymous with the word *arrival*.

14) The correct answer is A. The word *stringent* is synonymous with the word *strict*.

15) The correct answer is C. The author mentions that being on the road with automotive traffic is particularly dangerous for cyclists. Paragraph 2 states that seventy percent of fatal cycling accidents involved motor vehicles.

16) The correct answer is B. The author mentions deaths from cycling in paragraph 2 to emphasize the importance of bicycle safety. After mentioning the deaths, the author states "so it is of paramount importance that bicyclists take safety precautions to protect themselves."

17) The correct answer is B. The author mentions the adjustment of the helmet because many people wear it incorrectly and ineffectively. In paragraph 3 of the text, the author says: "The helmet is often worn incorrectly, thereby offering inadequate protection."

18) The correct answer is D. The author feels that failing to check cycling equipment is irresponsible. The first sentence of paragraph 3 says: "Cyclists would be imprudent not to check their equipment before setting out on any bike ride or journey." *Imprudent* and *irresponsible* are synonyms.

19) The correct answer is: having played. We need the perfect infinitive form *to have played*. We need to use this form after words like *claim* or *argue*.

20) The correct answer is: and. We need to use *but* instead of *and*, since we are contrasting the idea of the increase in funds against the idea of the increasing debt.

21) The correct answer is: having. We need to use the present simple form *has* instead since the rope and pulley is still in use today.

22) The correct answer is: principle. We need to use the word *principal* instead, because we are referring to the primary function of something, rather than a principle, which is an idea or theory.

23) The correct answer is B. We need the emphatic form with *do* in this sentence since the speaker is emphasizing the idea of being extra cautious.

24) The correct answer is B. We need to use the perfect infinitive *to have worked* because the speaker is describing a feeling that has relevance at the moment of speaking.

25) The correct answer is A. We are starting a new clause in the sentence, so we need to use *you and he* as the grammatical subject of the clause.

26) The correct answer is D. We need the passive form *be invited* since the friend is receiving the action of being invited, rather than doing the inviting.

27) The correct answer is A. This construction correctly uses the word *should* to express the obligation and also has the correct word order.

28) The correct answer is A. The main idea of the passage is that bees and flowers depend on each another. The text begins as follows:" Did you know that flowers and bees share a symbiotic relationship? Yes, that's right! Bees benefit from flowers, but flowers could not flourish without bees."

29) The correct answer is B. Bees benefit from flowers because they create food from flower pollen and nectar. This is mentioned in paragraphs 2 and 3.

30) The correct answer is D. Flowers and other plants need bees in order to develop seeds and duplicate. This is explained in paragraphs 4 and 5.

31) The correct answer is C. From the work of bees, human beings gain an increased selection of food. The text talks about fruits, vegetables, and other plant products in the last paragraph.

32) The correct answer is C. Nassir has named the following people in his planner for the month: Ali, Marta, Martin, Suki, Terri, Jacinta, Tom, and Jim, for a total of eight people.

33) The correct answer is B. Nassir typically goes to martial arts training at 7:00 or 8:00pm.

34) The correct answer is D. Nassir plans on personal training four times this month.

35) The correct answer is D. The note in the introductory information states: "His normal work schedule every week is from Monday to Friday, 8 am to 5 pm." So, Nassir only notes work hours that are outside his normal schedule.

36) The correct answer is D. The sentences are correct as written.

37) The correct answer is A. We need the present perfect tense *has decided* since we are describing a past action that is of current significance.

38) The correct answer is D. The sentence is correct as written.

39) The correct answer is A. The plans are definite, so we should use *will* instead of *would*. Remember to use *would* in hypothetical or uncertain situations.

40) The correct answer is A. The sentence is describing the time that something will take place, so *when* is needed rather than *which*.

41) The correct answer is C. The word *concerns* is plural, so the word *questions* should also be plural.

42) The correct answer is A. The grammatical subject of the sentence is *they* and the main verb is the word *are*.

43) The correct answer is B. *Being caring* is a gerund that forms the grammatical subject of the sentence, while the main verb is the word *is*.

44) The correct answer is B. *Reading and swimming* is a gerund phrase that forms the grammatical subject of the sentence, while the main verb is the word *are*.

45) The correct answer is C. In both sentences, the word *trade* is used an as adjective to refer to international commerce. Sentence A uses the word as a verb, while sentences B and D use the word as a noun.

46) The correct answer is C. The word *scratch* in these sentences is used as a verb to refer to the action of using the fingernails to relieve the sensation of itching. The word is used as a noun in sentences A and D, while sentence C uses the word in its metaphorical sense.

47) The correct answer is A. In these sentences, the word *produce* is used as a noun to refer to fresh fruit and vegetables. The word is used as a verb in the other sentences.

48) The correct answer is D. This sentence shows the correct chronological sequence of events.

49) The correct answer is C. This is the only sentence that conveys the events in the correct order of cause and effect.

50) The correct answer is A. This sentence correctly sets up the contrast between giving a message of deterrence and granting the lenient sentence.

Printed in the USA
CPSIA information can be obtained
at www.ICGtesting.com
LVHW052008260923
759374LV00011B/923